EGYPTIAN PRO

Third Edition

Expanded with More Proverbs, a new Bibliography and Index

Cruzian Mystic Books
P.O.Box 570459
Miami, Florida, 33257
(305) 378-6253 Fax: (305) 378-6253

First U.S. edition 1996

The author is available for group lectures and individual counseling. For further information contact the publisher.

Ashby, Muata
Egyptian Proverbs ISBN: 1-884564-00-3

Library of Congress Cataloging in Publication Data

1 Egyptian Philosophy 2 African Mythology 3 Meditation, 4 Self Help.

Cruzian Mystic Books

Other Books by Muata Ashby

Muata Ashby is the author of over 20 books on Yoga, Ancient Egypt, Meditation, Maat Philosophy, Christianity and more.

See the back section of this book for a complete listing.

All praises to the Divine for bringing salvation to the world through the words of wisdom!

ABOVE LEFT: The Ancient Egyptian God Djehuti-called Thoth, Hermes or Asclapius by the Greeks.

He is the creator of hieroglyphic writing and music as well as medical science.

ABOVE RIGHT: The Ancient Egyptian Goddess Sesheta. She is the goddess of writing and wisdom and an aspect of the great Ancient Egyptian goddesses Maat and Aset (Isis).

TABLE OF CONTENTS

INTRODUCTION

This new volume of "Egyptian Proverbs: TemTTchaas" is a revised and indexed version of a previous work entitled "TemTTchaas: Egyptian Proverbs. The new subject headings were designed to make it easier to find specific proverbs. Also, we have added an introduction giving a brief explanation of Maat Philosophy and new images to complement the teachings given in the text as well as a section on how to begin meditation.

What is Maat?

The Philosophy of Maat is perhaps the oldest known philosophy of righteous action which when followed and understood to perfection, leads to spiritual evolution in the individual human being as well as the society which practices it. Originating in ancient Egypt prior to 5,500 BCE, the philosophy of MAAT is symbolized by a goddess who is the daughter of the Supreme Being (Ra), creator of the Cosmos. MAAT herself is "the foundation of the Cosmos" and MAAT symbolizes: Truth, Justice, Order, Regularity, etc. Therefore, those who live a life based on truth, that is, with these virtues, will come into harmony with MAAT and thus the Universe itself and thereby with God as well. In this harmony, true happiness is to be found. Those who act in discord with MAAT, that is, those who live un-righteously and in disharmony with nature (the neters -divine cosmic forces) will suffer the consequences of their actions as dictated by the law of a cause and effect (Meskhenet - Karma). They will be subject to experience the judgment of their un-righteous actions from their own Higher Self.*

By living a life based on wisdom and truth, one can discover the divinity of the soul, its union to the universe, the supreme peace and contentment which comes from satisfying the inner drive for self discovery. Those who live a life based on mental agitation, greed, anger, hatred, confusion, lust, etc. will not discover their divine nature and will become more separated from their divine essence. Further, they will become more engaged with their own egoistic thoughts and suffer the pains and sorrows of human existence without being able to discover Hetep (Supreme Peace).

The simplicity and beauty of MAAT affords everyone, regardless of age, gender, country of origin or religious affiliation, an opportunity to partake in the promise of spiritual emancipation. MAAT is not only a philosophy of right action and harmony with the universe but it is also a mythology which has been ritualized and codified into the *Egyptian Book of Coming Forth By Day*. In this book the soul of the person is judged by his/her own deeds and actions (***Meskhenet* - Karma)**. If the Heart is found to be light, that is, free of burdens and heaviness of sorrow, worries and desires due to wrong living, then it is allowed to progress further in order to discover its essential nature as one with the Divine, that is to say, into the light of Day. If it is found to be heavier than the feather of MAAT, then it is consumed in the hell fires of its own creation, i.e. it experiences the pain and sorrow of unfulfilled desires, and eventually reincarnates on earth once again.* Thus, MAAT is a spiritual philosophy which promotes the evolution of the soul through right understanding and right action.

How to use this book:

The teachings of wisdom and spiritual life have been arranged in the format prescribed by the Temple of Isis. The teachings of spiritual life and the process of their instruction should be carried out as described below.

The spiritual aspirant needs to engage in the following process of spiritual practice:

1- Listening to the teachings.
2- Constant study and reflection on the teachings along with practicing them in everyday life situations.
3- Meditation on the meaning of the teachings.

Therefore, this book has been arranged in three parts: Part I describes the teachings of wisdom related to spiritual truths and the nature of the human soul. Part II describes how to better understand, practice and live by the teachings. Part III describes how to meditate on the wisdom teachings.*

As a study group resource - choose a particular proverb, then remaining in silence for 5 minutes, individually reflect on its meaning. Then each individual should state his/her understanding of the proverb and then the group may openly discuss its meaning.
- bring up your personal experiences in reference to the proverb and discuss ways to practice it in daily life.

As a meditation resource - choose a particular proverb and meditate on it. Then reflect on it throughout the day or for a week. Allow its wisdom to become a part of your every thought and day to day activity. Gradually it will become a part of you and every act will become righteous and divine.

How to practice MAAT:

Practicing the philosophy of MAAT means a gradual "becoming" process. "Becoming" implies that one transforms oneself through one's actions from an egoistic personality into a source of universal peace and caring for all humanity. Through your study of this volume you will discover that Maat Philosophy involves the following practices:

-studying the wisdom teachings,
-selfless service,
-wisdom in action (Karma Yoga),
-dedication of all actions to the Divine as a form of Devotional Love.

These dynamic elements are to be practiced in everyday life. Their practice serves to purify the heart (conscious, subconscious and unconscious levels of mind) so as to render it subtle and clear of complexes and agitation. When this purification process reaches a high degree of perfection, the human soul unites with the Universal Soul or God, who is the source of Supreme Peace - HETEP.

*For more on this teaching it is recommended that you read the book Egyptian Yoga by the same author.

How to study the wisdom teachings:

There is a specific technique which is prescribed by the scriptures themselves for studying the teachings, proverbs and aphorisms of mystical wisdom. The method is as follows:

The spiritual aspirant should read the desired text thoroughly, taking note of any particular teachings which resonates with him or her.

The aspirant should make a habit of collecting those teachings and reading them over frequently. The scriptures should be read and re-read because the subtle levels of the teachings will be increasingly understood the more the teachings are reviewed.

One useful exercise is to choose some of the most special teachings you would like to focus on and place them in large type or as posters in your living areas so as to be visible to remind you of the teaching.

The aspirant should discuss those teachings with others of like mind when possible because this will help to promote greater understanding and act as an active spiritual practice in which the teachings are kept at the forefront of the mind. in this way, the teachings can become an integral part of everyday life and not reserved for a particular time of day or of the week.

The study of the wisdom teachings should be a continuous process in which the teachings become the predominant factor of life rather than the useless and oftentimes negative and illusory thoughts of those who are ignorant of spiritual truths. This spiritual discipline should be observed until Enlightenment is attained.

May you discover supreme peace in this very lifetime!

MUATA ⊙

EGYPTIAN PROVERBS

(HETEP - Supreme Peace)

About Ancient Egypt:

"Ancient KMT is the Image of Heaven and the Shrine of the World."

"KMT"
"Egypt", "Burnt", "Land of Blackness", "Land of the Burnt People."

"India taken as a whole, beginning from the north and embracing what of it is subject to Persia, is a continuation of Egypt and the Ethiopians."

The Itinerarium Alexandri A.C.E. 345

"There are Egyptian columns as far off as NYASA, Arabia... Isis and Osiris led an army into India, to the source of the Ganges, and as far as the Indus Ocean."

Recorded by Egyptian High Priest *Manetho* (300 B.C.) and *Diodorus* (Greek historian 100 B. C.)

ABOUT THE ANCIENT EGYPTIANS:

"Our people originated at the base of the mountain of the Moon, at the origin of the Nile river."†

"They also say that the Egyptians are colonists sent out by the Ethiopians, Osiris having been the leader of the colony."

Diodorus Siculus

"When therefore, you hear the myths of the Egyptians concerning the Gods - wanderings and dismemberings and many such passions, think none of these things spoken as they really are in state and action. For they do not call Hermes "Dog" as a proper name, but they associate the watching and waking from sleep of the animal who by Knowing and not Knowing determines friend from foe with the most Logos-like of the Gods."

Plutarch

"The Egyptians and Nubians have thick lips, broad noses, woolly hair and burnt skin...
...And the Indian tribes I have mentioned, their skins are all of the same color, much like the Ethiopians... their country is a long way from Persia towards the south..."

Herodotus

"The riches of Egypt are for the foreigners therein."

Anonymous Arabic proverb.

"Truly at weaving wiles the Egyptians are clever."

Anonymous

The Ethiopians and Egyptians are very black."

Aristotle

"Compared with the Egyptians, the Greeks are childish mathematicians."

Plato

"And upon his return to Greece, they gathered around and asked, "tell us about this great land of the Blacks called Ethiopia." And Herodotus said, "There are two great Ethiopian nations, one in Sind (India) and the other in Egypt."

Recorded by Diodorus (Greek historian 100 B.C.)

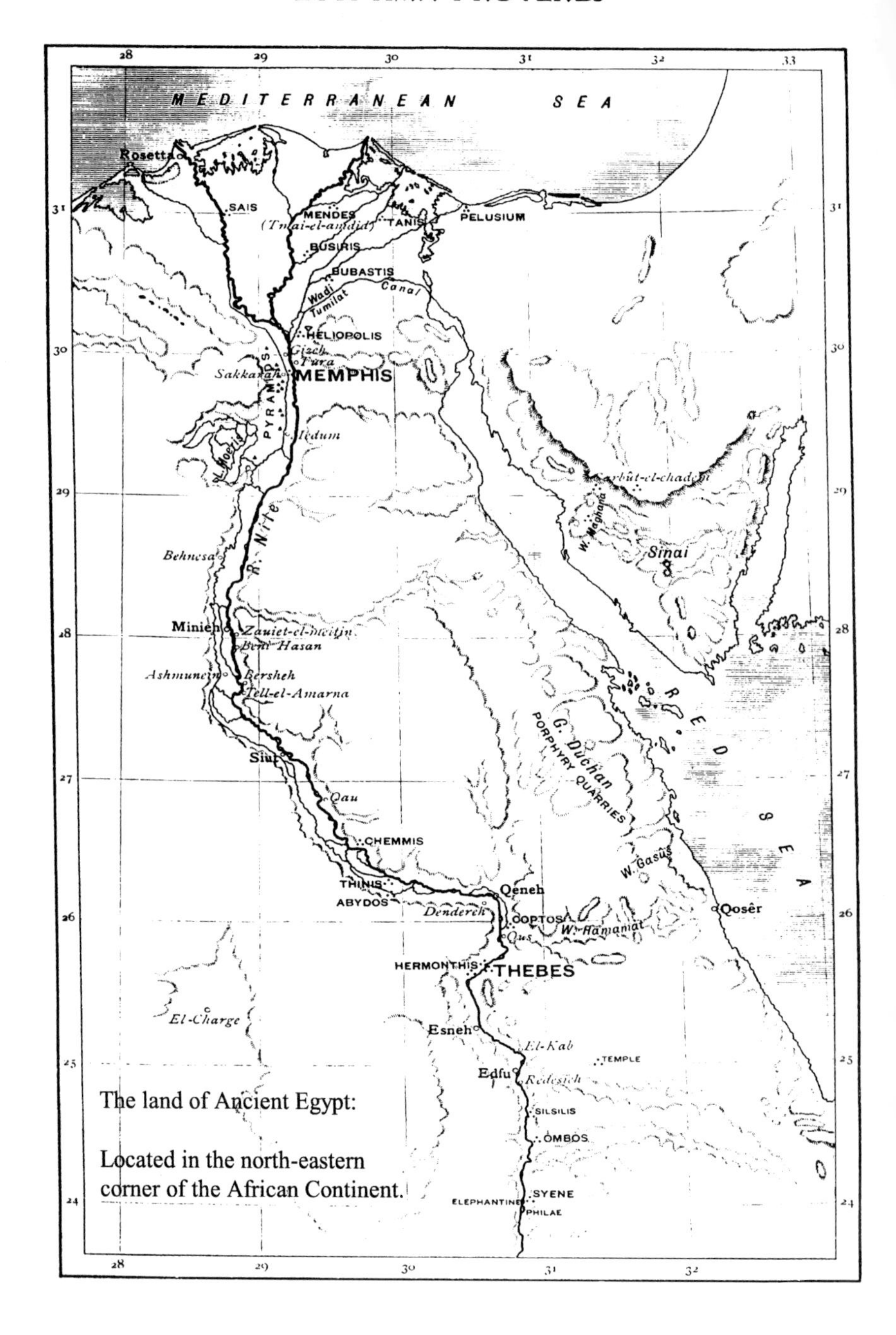

The land of Ancient Egypt:

Located in the north-eastern corner of the African Continent.

EGYPTIAN PROVERBS

Opening prayers:

O Åmen, O Åmen, who art in heaven, turn thy face upon the dead body of the child, and make your child sound and strong in the Underworld.

O Åmen, O Åmen, O God, O God, O Åmen, I adore thy name, grant you to me that I may understand thee; Grant you that I may have peace in the Duat, and that I may possess all my members therein...

Hail, Åmen, let me make supplication unto thee, for I know thy name, and thy transformations are in my mouth, and thy skin is before my eyes. Come, I pray thee, and place you thine heir and thine image, myself, in the everlasting underworld... let my whole body become like that of a neter, let me escape from the evil chamber and let me not be imprisoned therein; for I worship thy name..

"LET NOT BE SHUT IN MY SOUL, LET NOT BE FETTERED MY SHADOW, LET BE OPENED THE WAY FOR MY SOUL AND FOR MY SHADOW, MAY IT SEE THE GREAT GOD. MAY I LOOK UPON MY SOUL AND MY SHADOW"

—From the Ancient Egyptian
Hymns of Amun

These utterances (hekau) shall be recited by a person purified and washed; one who has not eaten animal flesh or fish.

And behold, these things shall be performed by one who is clean, and is ceremonially pure, a man who hath eaten neither meat nor fish, and who hath not had sexual.

—From The Ancient Egyptian Book of Coming Forth by Day

PART I
LISTENING TO THE WISDOM TEACHINGS

EGYPTIAN PROVERBS

ON MAAT

"MAAT is great and its effectiveness lasting; it has not been disturbed since the time of Osiris. There is punishment for those who pass over it's laws, but this is unfamiliar to the covetous one....When the end is nigh, *MAAT* lasts."

"Those who live today will die tomorrow, those who die tomorrow will be born again; Those who live MAAT will not die."

"No one reaches the beneficent West (heaven) unless their heart is righteous by doing *MAAT*. There is no distinction made between the inferior and the superior person; it only matters that one is found faultless when the balances and the two weights stand before the Lord of Eternity. No one is free from the reckoning. Thoth, a baboon, holds the balances to count each one according to what they have done upon earth."

"The sky is at peace, the earth is in joy, for they have heard that the King will set right the place of disorder. Tutankhamon drove out disorder from the Two Lands, and *MAAT* is firmly established in its place; he made lying an abomination, and the land is as it was at the first time."

"Speak *MAAT*; do *MAAT*."

"They who revere *MAAT* are *long lived*; they who are covetous have no tomb."

"Do *MAAT* for the King, for *MAAT* is that which God loves! Speak *MAAT* to the King for that which the King loves is *MAAT!"*

A great gift of God, is Maat.
Given, it is, only to those chosen by God.
The might of those who resemble God,
The poor are saved from their tormentor through it.

WHO IS GOD?

"God is one and alone, none other existeth with Him, God is One."

The One who has made all things.
GOD is a Spirit, a hidden Spirit, the Spirit of Spirits...The Divine Spirit."

"GOD is from the beginning and He has been from the beginning, GOD existed from old and was, before anything else had being. GOD existed when nothing else existed, and what now exists, GOD created... Before creation, not was created the earth, not were created men, not were created the Gods,
not was created DEATH "

"GOD is the father of beings.
GOD is the eternal One...and infinite and endures for ever.
GOD is hidden and no man knows God's form.
No man has been able to seek out GOD's likeness.
GOD is hidden to Gods and men...GOD's name remains hidden...It is a mystery to his children (men, women, Gods) GOD's names are innumerable, manifold and no one knows their number."

"GOD is truth, and GOD has established the earth thereupon."

"GOD is life and through Him only Human kind lives. GOD gives life to men and women, breathing the breath of life into their nostrils."

"GOD is both Father and Mother, the Father of fathers and the Mother of mothers. He begets but was never begotten, produces but was never produced; He begat Himself and produced himself."
"GOD creates but was never created; He is the maker of his own form, and

the fashioner of His own body."

"GOD endures without increase or diminution.
GOD multiplies himself millions of times, and He is manifold in forms and members."

"GOD made the universe and all that is within.
GOD is the Creator of what is in this world and what was, what is and what will be."

"GOD is the Father of Gods; GOD fashioned men and formed the Gods."

"GOD is merciful unto those who reverence Him, and He hears they that call upon Him."

"GOD KNOWS they who acknowledge Him, GOD rewards them who serve Him and protects them who follow Him; they who
Set Him in their HEART"

At left: Egyptian Goddess of Truth, Justice and Righteous-ness: MAAT. Her symbols are the feather of the IBIS (Divine Word-Truth-Wisdom), Ankh (eternal life, Papyrus staph (writing instrument to incribe the law and result of the judgement of the heart.).

EGYPTIAN PROVERBS

"GOD's RAYS are the guides of millions of men and women."

"GOD gives the whole earth unto those who love Him.
Gods and Goddesses bow down in adoration before GOD's soul."

"GOD is more hidden than all the Gods."

"The (Sun) Disk is his symbol but GOD." ☉

"Neter (GOD) is in the self or nowhere else, if it is found in the self it will be found EVERYWHERE"

"There is only one SUPREME BEING; ALL is IT; IT manifests itself in infinite forms and many Gods."

"Under, and back of, the Universe of Time and Space and Change, is ever to be found The Substantial Reality: the Fundamental Truth."

"That which is the Fundamental Truth, the Substantial Reality, is beyond true naming, but the Wise men call it The All."

"In its essence, The ALL is Unknowable."

"The Universe is Mental, held in the mind of The ALL. The ALL is SPIRIT"

"I became from God one God(s) three.

EGYPTIAN PROVERBS

"The infinite mind of The ALL is the womb of Universes"

"The ALL creates in its Infinite Mind, countless Universes, which exist for eons of time, to The All, the creation, development and death of a million Universes is as the time of the twinkling of an eye."

"Within the Father-Mother mind of The ALL, mortal children are at home."

"While ALL is in THE ALL, it is also true that THE ALL is in ALL. To him who truly understands this truth hath come great knowledge."

"It casts Its eye toward the clouds, finds it not the heavens full of It's wonders? It looks down on earth, does not the worm proclaim "Less than omnipotence could not have formed me!"

"But The ALL Father-Mother Mind being male and female and Life and Light, did bring forth Man co-equal to Him-Her self, with whom She fell in love, as being His own child; for he was beautiful beyond compare, the Image of her Sire. In very truth God fell in love with Her own Form; and on him did he bestow all of His own formations."

"God is not Mind, but Cause that the Mind is; God is not Spirit, but Cause that Spirit is; God is not Light; but Cause that Light is."

"Spirit pervading the body, by means of veins, arteries and blood, gives the living creature motion, and as it were does bear it in a way."

"The Good is the one who gives all things and naught receives. God, then, is Good and Good is God. The rest of the immortal ones are honored with the name of God, and spoken of as Gods; but God is Good not out of courtesy but out of nature. For God's nature and the Good are one; one is the kind of both, from which all other kinds proceed. Though, then, Good is spoken of by all, it is not understood by all, what thing It is."

"There are two images of God-Cosmos and Humankind."

"Yes, understand what God, what The Cosmos is and what is a life that cannot die, and what is a life subject to dissolution: the Cosmos is by God and in God, but Man by Cosmos and in Cosmos. The Cosmos is the first of living things, man is second after it, though first of things subject to death. The source and limit and constitution of all things is God."

"Not known are the things which will do God."

You have made millions of creations from thy One self (viz.) towns and cities, villages, fields, roads and river. Every eye (i.e., all men) beholds thee confronting it. You art the Aton of the day at its zenith.

ON SELF KNOWLEDGE

"KNOW THYSELF"

"Self knowledge is the basis of true knowledge."

"The noblest employment of the mind is the study of it's Creator."

EGYPTIAN PROVERBS

"Those who have learned to know themselves, have reached that state which does transcend any abundance of physical existence; but they who through a love that leads astray, expend their love upon their body, they stay in darkness, wandering and suffering through their senses, things of anxiety, unrest and Death."

A Devotee of ISIS is:

"One who ponders over sacred matters and seeks therein for hidden truth."

"Salvation is the freeing of the soul from its bodily fetters; becoming a God through knowledge and wisdom; controlling the forces of the cosmos instead of being a slave to them; subduing the lower nature and through awakening the higher self, ending the cycle of rebirth and dwelling with the Neters who direct and control the Great Plan."

"It is a misfortune to be a soldier, and a misery to till the ground, for the only happiness for mankind is to turn the heart to books during the daytime and to read during the night."

"If you seek God, you seek for the Beautiful. One is the Path that leads unto It - Devotion joined with Knowledge."

"Mastery of self consists not in abnormal dreams, visions and fantastic imaginings or living, but in using the higher FORCES against the lower thus escaping the pains of the lower by vibrating on the higher."

EGYPTIAN PROVERBS

"The purpose of all human life is to achieve a state of consciousness apart from bodily concerns."

"Develop the life giving fire; few know how to use it and fewer how to master it. Master the fire of the back and you will have mastered Seth."

"Men and women are to become God-like through a life of virtue and the cultivation of the spirit through scientific knowledge, practice and bodily discipline."

"Salvation is the freeing of the soul from its bodily fetters; becoming a God through knowledge and wisdom; controlling the forces of the cosmos instead of being a slave to them; subduing the lower nature and through awakening the higher self, ending the cycle of rebirth and dwelling with the Neters who direct and control the Great Plan."

"Know thyself as the pride of creation, the link uniting divinity and matter; behold a part of God Itself within thee; remember thine own dignity nor dare descend to evil or meanness."

"Make your life the subject of intense inquiry, in this way you will discover its goal, direction, and destiny."

"To free the spirit, control the senses; the reward will be a clear insight."

EGYPTIAN PROVERBS

"Know that what sees in thee and hears, is the Lord's Word; but Mind is Father-Mother God. Not separate are they the one from the other; just in their union does Life consist."

"To Know God, strive to grow in stature beyond all measure; conceive that there is nothing beyond thy capability. Know thyself deathless and able to know all things, all arts, sciences, the way of every life. Become higher than the highest height and lower than the lowest depth. Amass in thyself all senses of animals, fire, water, dryness and moistness. Think of thyself in all places at the same time, earth, sea, sky, not yet born, in the womb, young, old, dead, and in the after death state."

"The Mind being builder does use the fire as tool for the construction of all things, but that of man only for things on earth. Stripped of its fire the mind on earth cannot make things divine, for it is human in it's dispensation. And such a Soul, when from the body freed, if it have fought the fight of piety-to Know God and to do wrong to no one-such Soul becomes entirely mind. Whereas the impious Soul remains in it's own essence, chastised by its own self."

"Those who hath learned to know themselves, hath reached that Good which does transcend abundance; but they who through a love that leads astray, expend their love upon their body; they stay in Darkness wandering, and suffering through their senses things of Death."

"Indeed they who are yonder (those who live righteously will join GOD after death), will be living Gods, punishing anyone who commits a sin. Indeed they who are yonder will stand in the boat (barke of RA) causing the choicest offerings in it to be given to the temples. Indeed he who is yonder will become a sage who will not be hindered from appealing to GOD whenever they speak."

"If you seek GOD, you seek for the Beautiful. One is the Path that leads unto GOD - Devotion joined with knowledge."

"As the ocean gives rise to springs, whose water return again into the bosom through the rivers, so runs thy life force from the heart outwards, and so returns into its place again."

"God sheds light on they who shake the clouds of Error from their soul, and sight the brilliancy of Truth, mingling themselves with the All-sense of the Divine Intelligence, through love of which they win their freedom from that part over which Death rules, and has the seed of the assurance of future Deathlessness implanted in him. This, then, is how the good will differ from the bad."

"The path of immortality is hard, and only a few find it. The rest await the Great Day when the wheels of the universe shall be stopped and the immortal sparks shall escape from the sheathes of substance. Woe unto those who wait, for they must return again, unconscious and unknowing, to the seed-ground of stars, and await a new beginning."

"Whoever has eaten the knowledge of every God, their existence is for all eternity and everlasting in their spirit body; what they will they do."

"If then you learn that you art thyself of Life and Light, and that you only happen to be out of them, You shalt return again to Life."

"Unless you first hate your Body, you cannot love your Self. But if you love your Self, you shall have INTELLECT, and having INTELLECT you shall share in the KNOWLEDGE. KNOWLEDGE will lead to love and love to salvation."

EGYPTIAN PROVERBS

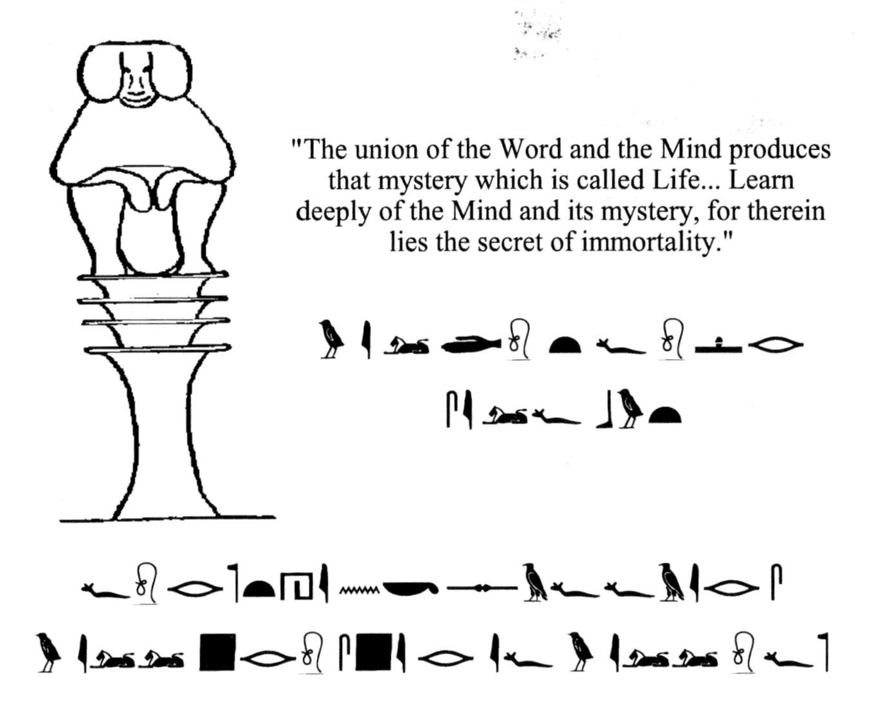

"The union of the Word and the Mind produces that mystery which is called Life... Learn deeply of the Mind and its mystery, for therein lies the secret of immortality."

"You shall exist for millions of millions of years."

"Soul to heaven, body to earth."

"Nothing in Heaven is a slave; nothing on earth is free."

"A Soul, when from the body freed, if it has fought the fight of piety- to Know God and to do wrong to no one such a Soul becomes entirely pure. Whereas the impious Soul remains as it is, a slave to its passions, chastised through death, by its own self."

"There is not one who is Fatherless nor Motherless in the Universe."

"There can be no more righteous piety than to know the things that are and to give thanks to Father-Mother God who made them; Who gives thanks is pious; the pious will get to know both where is truth and what it is."

The 10 VIRTUES of the Initiates:

(1)"Control your thoughts,"

(2)"Control your actions,"

(3)"Have devotion of purpose,"

(4)"Have faith in your master's ability to lead you along the path of truth,"

(5)"Have faith in your own ability to accept the truth,"

(6)"Have faith in your ability to act with wisdom,"

(7)"Be free from resentment under the experience of persecution,"

(8)"Be free from resentment under experience of wrong,"

(9)"Learn how to distinguish between right and wrong,"

(10)"Learn to distinguish the real from the unreal."

"Thinking, understanding, reasoning, willing, call not these Soul! They are its actions, but they are not its essence."

"Learn to see clearly, learn to wish for what is just, learn to dare what your conscience dictates, learn to keep your intentions a secret, and if, despite all your efforts, today brings no more than yesterday, do not lose courage, but continue steadfastly, keeping your goal before you with determination. Onward! The SEVEN COMPANIONS of the SOUL-the planetary spirits-guard the secret key which locks the past and opens the future. Let your efforts be aimed at the CROWN of the MASTER."

PART II STUDY AND REFLECTION ON THE TEACHINGS

The Precepts of MAAT

(1) "DO N0T INIQUITY."

(2) "DO NOT ROB WITH VIOLENCE."

(3) "DO NO VIOLENCE (TO ANY ONE OR ANYTHING)."

(4) "DO NOT COMMIT THEFT."

(5) "DO NOT MURDER MAN OR WOMAN."

(6) "DO NOT DEFRAUD OFFERINGS."

(7) "DO NOT ACT DECEITFULLY."

(8) "DO NOT ROB THE THINGS THAT BELONG TO GOD."

(9) "TELL NO LIES."

(10) "DO NOT SNATCH AWAY FOOD FROM THE NEEDY."

(11) "DO NOT UTTER EVIL WORDS."

(12) "DO NOT ATTACK ANY ONE."

(13) "DO NOT SLAUGHTER THE CATTLE THAT ARE SET APART FOR THE GODS."

(14) "DO NOT EAT YOUR HEART".

(15) "DO NOT LAY WASTE THE PLOUGHED LANDS."

(16) "DO NOT BE AN EAVESDROPPER OR PRY INTO MATTERS TO MAKE MISCHIEF."

(17) "DO NOT SPEAK AGAINST ANYONE."

(18) "DO NOT ALLOW YOURSELF TO BECOME ANGRY WITHOUT CAUSE."

(19) "DO NOT COMMIT ADULTERY."

(20) "DO NOT COMMIT ANY SIN AGAINST YOUR OWN PURITY."

(21) "DO NOT VIOLATE SACRED TIMES AND SEASONS."

(22) "DO NOT DO THAT WHICH IS ABOMINABLE."

(23) "DO NOT UTTER FIERY WORDS. DO NOT BE A MAN OR WOMAN OF ANGER."

(24) "DO NOT STOP YOUR EARS AGAINST THE WORDS OF RIGHT AND WRONG."

(25) "DO NOT STIR UP STRIFE." "DO NOT CAUSE TERROR." DO NOT STRIKE FEAR INTO ANYONE"

(26) "DO NOT CAUSE ANY ONE TO WEEP."

(27) "DO NOT LUST OR COMMIT FORNICATION NOR LAY WITH OTHERS OF YOUR SAME SEX."
(28) "DO NOT AVENGED YOURSELF."

(29) "DO NOT WORK GRIEF, DO NOT ABUSE ANY ONE."

(30) "DO NOT ACT INSOLENTLY OR WITH VIOLENCE."

(31) "DO NOT JUDGE HASTILY."

(32) "DO NOT TRANSGRESS OR ANGER GOD."

(33) "DO NOT MULTIPLY YOUR SPEECH OVERMUCH."

(34) "DO NOT HARM OR EVIL."

(35) "DO NOT WORK TREASON OR CURSES ON THE KING."

(36) "NEVER BEFOUL THE WATER."

(37) "DO NOT SPEAK SCORNFULLY."

(38) "DO NOT CURSE THE GOD."

(39) "DO NOT BEHAVE WITH ARROGANCE."

(40) "DO NOT BE OVERWHELMINGLY PROUD OR SEEK FOR DISTINCTIONS."

(41) "DO NOT MAGNIFY YOUR CONDITION BEYOND WHAT IS FITTING OR INCREASE YOUR WEALTH, EXCEPT WITH SUCH THINGS AS ARE (JUSTLY) YOUR OWN POSSESSIONS."

(42) "DO NOT THINK EVIL OF OR SLIGHT THE GOD IN YOUR NATIVE TOWN."

ON INTEGRITY

"Go not in and out of court that thy name may not stink."

"The way to gain a good reputation is to endeavor to be what you desire to appear."

ON HONOR

"Honor is the inner garment of the soul; the first thing put on by it with the flesh, and the last it lays down at its separation from it."

"The higher the sun rises, the less shadow does he cast; even so the greater is the goodness, the less does it covet praise; yet cannot avoid its rewards in honors."

ON BEHAVIOR

"As a plain garment best adorns a beautiful person, so decent behavior is the best ornament of inner wisdom."

Set your goodness before people, Then you are greeted by all

Don't act with evil, kindness is an expression of good nature,
Make your memory last through love of you.

ON IMMATURITY

"You Greeks are but children."

ON THE NATURE OF THE SOUL

"Souls, Horus, son, are of the self-same nature, since they came from the same place where the Creator modeled them; nor male nor female are they. Sex is a thing of bodies not of Souls."

EGYPTIAN PROVERBS

You are The Supreme Being, who did create beings endowed with reason; you make the color of the skin of one race to be different from that of another, but, however many may be the varieties of mankind, it is you that make them all to live.

You (God) set every person in his place. You provide their daily food, every man having the portion allotted to him; [you] do compute the duration of his life. Their tongues are different in speech, their characteristics (or forms), and likewise their skins (in color), giving distinguishing marks to the dwellers in foreign lands... You make the life of all remote lands.

ON TRUTH

"The truth shall set you free"

"The laws of God are the first thing the seeker will find on the way to the truth."
"Truth is the great support of God"

"Truth and knowledge produce courage."

"The word which appeared as a pillar of flame out of the darkness is the Son of God, born of the mystery of the Mind. The name of the Word is Reason. Reason is the offspring of Thought and Reason shall divide the light from the darkness and establish Truth in the midst of the waters."

"The closer you get to the truth, the simpler it is"

"Truth is not simple except to those who know everything"

"O you who are enamored with the beauties of Truth, and have fixed thy heart on the simplicity of her charms, hold fast thy fidelity unto her, and forsake her not: the constancy of thy virtue shall crown thee with honor."

"Truth is but one; thy doubts are of thine own raising. It that made virtues what they are, planted also in thee a knowledge of their pre-eminence. Act as Soul dictates to thee, and the end shall be always right."

"Are not the enemies made by truth, better than the friends obtained by flattery?"

ON SLEEP AND WAKEFULNESS

"The sleep of the body is the sober watchfulness of the mind and the shutting of my eyes reveals the true Light."

"Body's sleep becomes the Soul's awakening, and closing of the eyes - true vision; pregnant with good my silence, and the utterance of my word begetting good things."

"The day time of the body is the night time of the soul; the night time of the body is the daytime of the Soul."

Awaken yourself, you who are Heru! Rise up against Set! Raise yourself and Asar, as a spirit Divine, as the son of Geb, being his first born, arise as Anpu and be the object of adoration for all!

ON PROSPERITY AND ADVERSITY

"Presume not in prosperity, neither despair in adversity: court not dangers, nor meanly fly from before them."

"Adversity is the seed of well doing; it is the nurse of heroism and boldness; who that hath enough, will endanger himself to have more? Who that is at ease, will set their life on the hazard?

"Neither let prosperity put out the eyes of circumspection, nor abundance cut off the hands of frugality; they that too much indulge in the superfluities of life, shall live to lament the want of its necessaries."

"See that prosperity elate not thine heart above measure; neither adversity depress thine mind unto the depths, because fortune beareth hard against you. Their smiles are not stable, therefore build not thy confidence upon them; their frowns endure not forever, therefore let hope teach you patience."

"When opulence and extravagance are a necessity instead of righteousness and truth, society will be governed by greed and injustice."

One man is rich, another is poor,
But food remains for him who shares it.
As to him who was rich last year,
He is a vagabond this year;
Don't be greedy to fill your belly,
You don't know your end at all.
Should you come to be in want,
Another may do good to you.
When last year's watercourse is gone,
Another river is here today.

"When sight and hearing fail the many, those who cannot speak will lead."

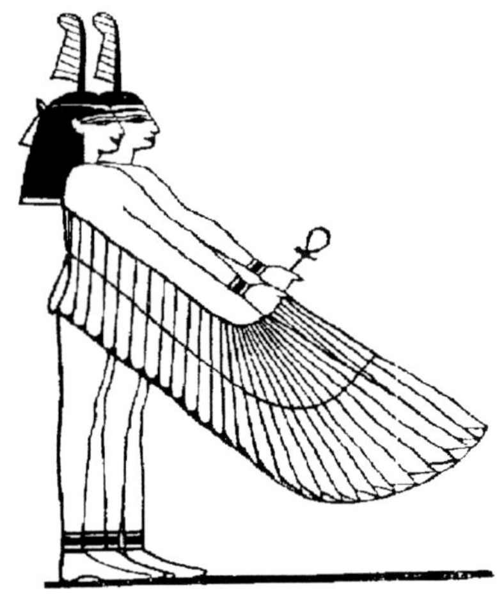

ON EVOLUTION

"All develops upward, anything that opposes the upward movement is destroyed."

EGYPTIAN PROVERBS

ON FORTITUDE

"As a camel bears labor, and heat, and hunger, and thirst, through deserts of sand, and faints not; so the fortitude of a man shall sustain him through perils."

ON THE RELATIONSHIP BETWEEN WOMAN AND MAN

"When you find sensibility of heart, joined with softness of manners, an accomplished mind, with a form agreeable to thy fancy, take her home to thy house; she is worthy to be thy friend, thy companion in life, the wife of thy bosom."

"Remember you art man's reasonable companion, not the slave of his passion; the end of thy being is not merely to gratify his loose desire, but to assist him in the toils of life, to soothe him with thy tenderness, and recompense his care and like treatment with soft endearments."

"If you take for a wife a good time woman who is joyful and who is well known in the town, if she is fickle and seems to live for the moment, do not reject her. Let her eat. The joyful person brings happiness."

"Beware of a woman or man from strange parts, whose city is not known. When they come, do not look at them nor know them. They are as the eddy in deep water, the depth of which is unknown. They whose spouse is far off writes to you every day. If no witness is near her they stand up and spread out their net: O! fearful crime to listen to them! Therefore, they who are wise avoid them and take to themselves a spouse in their youth; first, because one's own house is the best thing, and secondly, because an honest spouse will present you with a child like unto thyself."

"If you want friendship to endure in the house that you enter, the house of a master, of a brother or a friend, then in whatever place you enter beware of approaching the women there. Unhappy is the place where this is done. Unwelcome is he who intrudes on them. A thousand men are turned away from their good because of a short moment that is like a dream, and then that moment is followed by death that comes from having known that dream. Anyone who encourages you to take advantage of the situation gives you poor advice. When you go to do it your heart says no. If you are one who fails through the lust of women, then no affair of yours can prosper."

"When you prosper and establish your home, love your wife with ardor. Then fill her belly and clothe her back. Caress her. Give her ointments to soothe her body. Fulfill her wishes for as long as you live. She is a fertile field for her husband. Do not be brutal. Good manners will influence her better than force. Do not contend with her in the courts. Keep her from the need to resort to outside powers. Her eye is her storm when she gazes. It is by such treatment that she will be compelled to stay in your house."

"DO NOT commit adultery."

"DO NOT lust or commit fornication nor have lay with others of the same sex."

EGYPTIAN PROVERBS

ON THE INFINITY WITHIN

"Listen within yourself and look into the infinitude of Space and Time. There can be heard the songs of the Constellations, the voices of the Numbers, and the harmonies of the Spheres."

ON JUSTICE

"ISIS is blindfolded because justice is unprejudiced!"

"If you are an official of high standing, and you are commissioned to satisfy the many, then hold to a straight line. When you speak don't lean to one side or to the other. Beware lest someone complain, saying to the judges, "he has distorted things", and then your very deeds will turn into a judgment of you."

The one who has wealth at home will not be partial, He is a just man who lacks nothing.

ON LIGHT AND DARK

"I thy God am the Light and the Mind which were before substance was divided from Spirit, and darkness from Light."

"As the World is illuminated by the Sun, so is the human mind illuminated by that Light; nay, in fuller measure. But once the Divine sense hath been commingled with the human soul, there is at-one-ment from the happy union of the blending of their natures; so that minds of this kind are never more held fast in errors of the darkness."

ON WEALTH, SHARING, GIVING AND HAPPINESS

"If you be industrious to procure wealth, be generous in the disposal of it. One is never so happy as when giving happiness unto others."

"It is more difficult to be well with riches, than to be at ease under the want of them. Man governs himself much easier in poverty than in abundance."

"Follow your heart throughout your life. Do more than is required of you. Spend no more time on daily cares than required by your household, when wealth ultimately arrives, then too follow your heart for wealth does no good if you are downhearted."

"Those who give away their treasure wisely, gives away their plagues: they that retain their increase, heap up sorrow."

"The earth is barren of good things where she hoard up treasure; where gold is in her bowels, there no herb grows."

EGYPTIAN PROVERBS

"Help your friends with the things that you have, for you have these things by the grace of God. If you fail to help your friends, one will say "you have a selfish KA". One plans for tomorrow, but you do not know what tomorrow will bring. The right Soul is the Soul by which one is sustained. If you do praiseworthy deeds your friends will say "welcome" in your time of need."

"A noble spirit disdains the malice of fortune; its greatness of Soul is not to be cast down."

"The dastardly spirit of the timorous betrays them to shame. By shrinking under poverty, they stoop down to meanness; and by timely bearing insults they invent injuries.....In the hour of danger, they are embarrassed and confounded: in the day of misfortune they sink and despair overwhelm their Soul."

"Give bread to they who has no field, and create for thyself a good name for posterity for evermore."

"Labor not after riches first, and think you afterwards wilt enjoy them. He who neglects the present moment, throws away all that he hath. As the arrow passes through the heart, while the warrior knew not that it was coming; so shall his life be taken away before he knows that he hath it."

"If you are great after having been humble, if you have gained your wealth after having been poor, and then go to a town that you know and that knows your former condition, don't put your trust in your newly acquired wealth which has come to you as a gift of God. If you do, one day someone there who is poor may very well overtake you."

"Be generous as long as you live. What leaves the storehouse does not return. It is the food in the storehouse that one must share, that is coveted. One whose belly is empty becomes an opponent. Therefore, do not have an accuser or an opponent as a neighbor. Your kindness to your neighbors will be a memorial to you for years."

"Accept the authority of your leaders, then your house will endure in its wealth. Your rewards will come from the right place. Wretched are they who oppose their leader. One lives as long as one is mild. Baring your arm does not hurt it."

"Any riches you have are useless without the many."

"The Sun is the preserver and the nurse of every group. And just as the Intelligible Cosmos, holding the Sensible in it's embrace, fills it full, distending it with forms of every kind and every shape - so, too the Sun distendeth all in Cosmos, affording births to all, and strengtheneth them."

ON STEALING

"Do not plunder your neighbor's house or steal the goods of one that is near you, lest they denounce you before you are even heard."

EGYPTIAN PROVERBS

ON SPEECH

"If advice is given for the good, the great will speak accordingly. This is a matter of teaching a person to speak to posterity. He or she who hears it becomes a master hearer. It is good to speak to posterity. Posterity will listen."

"You, alone cannot speak. Wonder at thy glorious prerogative; and pay to the Supreme who gave to thee a rational and welcome praise, teaching thy children wisdom, instructing the offspring of thy loins in piety."

"Humanity is one; so speech is one, although the voice differs from race to race. The same speech may be found in Egypt, in Peoria and in Greece."

"If Mind and Divine Speech are used as meant, you will not differ from the immortals in any way."

ON INJUSTICE AND VIOLENCE

"Creating or allowing obstacles to the following of laws opens the way for violence."

Beware of punishing unjustly,
Do not kill anyone, it does not serve you or bring what you desire.
Punish instead with beatings, and detention,
By these actions the land will be well ordered.

"Punish firmly and chastise soundly, then repression of crime becomes an example. But punishment except for crime will turn the complainer into an enemy."

ON CONCENTRATION AND LIFE WORK OR OCCUPATION

"Do not disturb a great person or distract their attention when they are occupied, trying to understand their task. When they are thus occupied they strip their body through love of what they do. Love for the work which they do brings people closer to God. These are the people who succeed in what they do."

"Behold there is no profession which is not governed,
It is only the learned man who rules Himself"

"It is honor to thy nature when worthily employed, when you directs it to wrong purposes, it shames and destroy thee."

"All are not called to the guiding of the helm of state; neither are there armies to be commanded by every one; do well in that which is committed to thy charge, and praise shall remain upon thee."

ON THE FATE OF THE INCARNATED SOUL

"Perils, and misfortunes, and want, and pain, and injury, are more or less the certain lot of everyone that cometh into the world. It behooves thee, therefore, O child of calamity! early to fortify thy mind with courage and patience that you may support, with a becoming resolution, thy allotted portion of human evil."

ON THE FOOLISH AND THE WISE

"Speculation is the domain of the ignorant, to KNOW is the goal of the true SEEKER."

"As the moon retains her nature, though darkness spread itself before her face as a curtain, so the Soul remains perfect even in the bosom of the fool."

"The fool is not always unfortunate, nor the wise always successful, yet never has a fool thorough enjoyment; never was a wise person wholly unhappy."

If you are one among guests at the table of a person who is more powerful than you, take what that person gives just as it is set before you. Look at what is before you, do not stare at your host. Don't speak until spoken to; your words will then please the heart. The person of means acts as their KA commands; they will give to those who they favor; it is the KA that causes the arm to stretch out. The person of means gives to the chosen one; so eating is under the direction of God. It is a fool who complains about it."

"O fool, fool!, the pains which you take to hide what you art, are far more than would make thee what you would seem; and the children of wisdom shall mock at thy cunning when, in the midst of security, thy disguise is stripped off, and the finger of derision shall point thee to scorn."

"True wisdom is less presuming than folly. The wise person doubts often, and changes his mind; the fool is obstinate, and doubts not; knowing all but their own ignorance."

"The principles of truth are seven, he who knows these, understandingly, possesses the Magic Key before whose touch all the Doors of the Temple fly open."

"The wise person feeds the KA with what endures, so that it is happy with that person on earth. The wise is known by his or her wisdom. The great are known by their wisdom."

"The wise wake up early to their lasting gain while the fool is hard pressed."

"The heart of the wise matches his or her tongue and his or her lips are straight when he or she speaks."

"The wise have eyes that are made to see and ears that are made to hear what will profit the offspring."

EGYPTIAN PROVERBS

"The wise person who acts with MAAT is free of falsehood and disorder."

"The fool who does not hear, can do nothing at all; looking at ignorance and seeing knowledge; looking at harmfulness and seeing usefulness; living on the things by which one dies; the food of evil speech."

ON THE SPIRIT WORLD AND THE PHENOMENAL WORLD

"The visible world is ephemeral, the spirit world is forever; Gain strength from this since nothing physical can destroy you."

"There is no happiness for the soul in the external worlds since these are perishable, true happiness lies in that which is eternal, within us."

"The half wise, recognizing the comparative unreality of the universe, imagine they may defy its LAWS."

ON SERVICE

"The wise ones serve the higher planes and rule the lower, in this way one operates the laws instead being a slave to them."

ON SELFLESS SERVICE

Live upon truth,
Feed upon truth,
Perform the ordinances of men,
and the things which gratify the gods.
Propitiate the God by doing his will,
Given bread to the hungry man,
and water to him that was athirst,
and apparel to the naked man,
and a ferry boat to he who has no boat…

ON BUSINESS AND COMMERSE

Do not assess a man who has nothing,
And thus falsify your pen.
If you find a large debt against a poor man, Make it into three parts;
Forgive two, let one stand,
You will find it a path of life.

Haste not to be rich, but be not slothful in thine own interest.

One does not run to reach success,
One does not move to spoil it.

Don't make yourself a ferry on the river, And then strain to seek its fare;
Take the fare from him who is wealthy,
And let pass him who is poor.

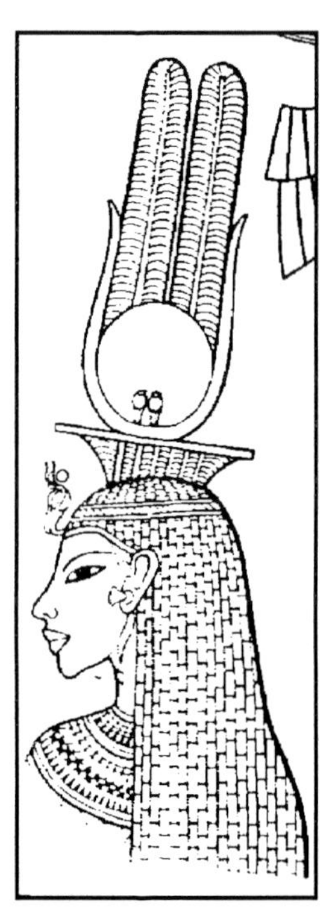

FROM: THE STELE OF ABU:

"Be chief of the mysteries at festivals, know your mouth, come in Hetep (peace), enjoy life on earth but do not become attached to it, it is transitory."

FROM THE STELE OF DJEHUTI-NEFER:

"Consume pure foods and pure thoughts with pure hands, adore celestial beings, become associated with wise ones: sages, saints and prophets; make offerings to GOD."

ON IGNORANCE, SLOTHFULNESS, VANITY, PRIDE AND EGOISM

"The wickedness of the soul is ignorance; the virtue of the soul is knowledge."

There is no darkness like the darkness of Ignorance"
"An infant's Soul is altogether a thing of beauty to see, not yet befouled by body's passions, still all but hanging from the Cosmic Soul! But when the body grows in bulk and draws down the Soul into it's mass, then does the Soul cut off itself and bring upon itself forgetfulness, and no more shares in the Beautiful and Good (God); and this forgetfulness becometh vice."

"Who is it that affirms most boldly? Who is it that holds his opinion most obstinately? Ever they who hath most ignorance; for they also have most pride."

"O people of the earth, men and women born and made of the elements, but with the spirit of the Divine within you, rise from your sleep of ignorance! Be sober and thoughtful. Realize that your home is not on the earth but in the Light. Why have you delivered yourselves unto death, having power to partake of immortality? Repent, and change your minds. Depart from the dark light and forsake corruption forever. Prepare to blend your souls with the Eternal Light."

"Ignorance is slavery, be it to others or to ones own vices, to become free from both so as to live in eternal happiness and to work to establish the will of Father-Mother GOD on earth is the sacred task."

"The wickedness of the soul is ignorance, the virtue of the soul is knowledge."

"For the ill of ignorance does pour over all the earth and overwhelm the soul that's battened down within the body, preventing it from finding Salvation."

"Anything built by humanity for its glorification will eventually fall."

After sleep, Indulge not in morning slumber while the day breaks majestically in the sky.
What can be compared to dawn and daybreak for beauty?
To what can the man who knows not the dawn be compared?
For whilst God is performing His splendid work that man is wallowing in slothfulness.

ON PAIN

"As joy is not without its alloy of pain, so neither is sorrow without its portion of pleasure."

"The impious Soul screams: I burn; I am ablaze; I know not what to cry or do; wretched me, I am devoured by all the ills that compass me about; alack, poor me, I neither see nor hear! This is the Soul's chastisement of itself. For the Mind of the man imposes these on the Soul."

ON SUFFERING

"Suffering in search of truth gives true meaning to the truth."

"To suffer, is a necessity entailed upon your nature, would you prefer that miracles should protect you from its lessons or shalt you repine, because it happened unto you, when lo it happened unto all? Suffering is the golden cross upon which the rose of the Soul unfolds."

ON HUMILITY

"HUMILITY is a greater virtue than defying death; it triumphs over vanity and conceit; conquer them in yourself first!"

Better is praise and love of men,
Than material wealth in your storehouse;
Better is bread with a happy heart,
Than wealth with vexation.

ON GOSSIPING AND EVIL SPEECH

Do not repeat calumny,
Nor should you listen to it,
It is the spouting of the hot-bellied.
Report a thing observed, not heard,
If it is negligible, don't say anything,
He who is before you recognizes worth.

Do not malign anyone,
Great or small, the Ba abhors it.

Do not bear witness with false words,
So as to brush aside a man by your tongue.
You will find it a path of life.

Guard your tongue from harmful speech,
Then you will be loved by others.
You will find your place in the Sanctuary, the House of God,

The words men say are one thing,
The deeds of The God are another.
Do not say: "I have done no wrong,"
And then strain to seek a quarrel;
The wrong belongs to The God...

The hothead incites citizens; He creates divisions among the young; If you see that people follow him,
Speak out against him before those who give council, Suppress the hothead, he is against harmony, The talker is a troublemaker for society. Your duty is to curb the multitude, and suppress its heat...

Do not listen to an official's reply indoors
In order to repeat it to another outside.
Do not let your word be carried outside,
Lest your heart be aggrieved.

Do not reveal your heart to a stranger,
He might use your words against you;
The noxious speech that came from your mouth,
He repeats it and you make enemies.
A man may be ruined by his tongue...

If you are skilled in the art of speech, you will prevail,
The tongue is [a leader or wise person's] sword;
Speaking rightly is more powerful than all fighting,
The skillful in speech (ethics-philosophy) cannot be overcome.

LAW OF CAUSE AND EFFECT (KARMA)

"Everything we do is sowing, and all of our experiences are harvests."

"Every cause has its Effect; every Effect has its Cause; everything happens according to Law; Chance is a name for Law unrecognized; there are many planes of causation, but nothing escapes the Law."

"O think not, bold man, because thy punishment is delayed, that the arm of God is weakened; neither flatter thyself with hopes that the Supreme winks at thy doings; Its eye pierces the secrets of every heart, and remembered are they for ever..."

"This instant is thine; the next is in the womb of futurity, and you know not what it may bring forth; maturity of the unborn is in the keeping of the Law. Each future state is that you has created in the present."

"The choice of the earthly condition is made by the soul itself, and very generally it differs from what it has been in the preceding term of life in this world. The cause is in him who makes the choice and *the divinity is without blame in the matter.* After the choice has been made, the "daimon" or guardian angel is allotted"

ON SELF-RELIANCE

"Don't rely exclusively on the oracle for guidance; sometimes it is necessary for us to live our lives for ourselves and not to lean too heavily on other minds who, after all, have their own thing to do. If the Gods in their wisdom see fit to deny us access to outer time, then it is usually because of some decision made by our own free will or spirit, maybe even prior to entering the body."

Stand up and throw of the earth that is on you and do away with those two arms of Sct that are behind you!

ON EXERCISING THE FACULTY OF REASON

"Those who gave thee a body, furnished it with weakness; but The ALL who gave thee Soul, armed thee with resolution. Employ it, and you art wise; be wise and you art happy."

ON MOODINESS AND DEPRESSION

"To change your mood or mental state, change your vibration."

"To destroy an undesirable rate of mental vibration, concentrate on the opposite vibration to the one to be suppressed."

"What is the source of sadness, but feebleness of the mind? What gives it power but the want of reason? Rouse yourself to the combat, and it quits the field before you strike."

ON THE WORSHIP OF THE DIVINE

"There is no life for the soul except in knowing, and no salvation but doing."

"Give thyself to GOD, keep you thyself daily for God; and let tomorrow be as today."

"What is loved by God is obedience; God hates disobedience."

"O behold with thine eye God's plans. Devote thyself to adore God's name. It is God who gives Souls to millions of forms, and God magnifies whosoever magnifies God."

ON THE DIFFERENCE BETWEEN KNOWLEDGE (GNOSIS) AND REASON (INTELLECT- INFORMATION ABOUT SOMETHING.)

"Knowledge is far different from sense. For sense is brought about by that which hath the mastery over us, while Knowledge is the end of science, and science is God's gift. All science is incorporeal, the instrument it uses being the Mind, just as the Mind employs the body."

"Though all men suffer fated things, those led by reason (guided by the intellect), do not endure suffering with the rest; but' since they've freed themselves from viciousness, not being bad, they do not suffer bad. Though having thought fornication or murder but not having committed these, the Mind-led man will suffer just as though he had committed fornication, and though he be no murderer, as though he had committed murder because there was will to commit these things."

ON RIGHT ACTION

"Be industrious, let thine eyes be open, lest you become a beggar, for the man that is idle cometh not to honor."

"Seek to perform your duties to your highest ability, this way your actions will be blameless."

"As the rose breaths sweetness from its own nature, so the heart of a benevolent person produces good works."

"Good things cease to be good in our wrong enjoyment of them. What nature meant to be pure sweetness, are then sources of bitterness to us; from such delights arise pain, from such joys, sorrows."

"Magic consists of KNOWING the correct, exact gesture, word, pronunciation, all at the correct time; if these are not so, the system will not work. Those who go against nature may do so for a short time, but will undergo the correction of nature at their own peril."

"Say not that honor is the child of boldness, nor believe you that the hazard of life alone can pay the price of it: it is not to the action that it is due, but to the manner of performing it."

"Morals are judged by deeds."

"They who have received some portion of God's gift, these, if judged by their deeds, have from death's bond won their release; for they embrace in their own Mind, all things, things on the earth, things in the heaven, and things above the heaven - if there be aught. They who do not understand, because they possess the aid of reason only and not Mind, are ignorant wherefore they have come into being and whereby, like irrational creatures, their makeup is in their feelings and their impulses, they fail in all appreciation of things which really are worth contemplation. These center all their thought upon the pleasures of the body and its appetites."

"If you are mighty and powerful, then gain respect through knowledge and through your gentleness of speech. Don't order things except as it is fitting. The one who provokes others gets into trouble. Don't be haughty lest you be humbled. But also, don't be mute lest you be chided."

"He who is wrong fights against himself. "

"When sent as an emissary between people of great means, be careful to relay the true essence of the message and guard against provocative speech that angers such people. Stay with the truth. If the message was given to you with outburst, do not repeat the outburst, for maligning others is abhorred by the KA."

EGYPTIAN PROVERBS

"Live life, and not shall you die."

"Bend thy back before thy chief."

"Those who gave thee a body, furnished it with weakness; but The ALL who gave thee Soul, armed thee with resolution. Employ it, and you art wise; be wise and you art happy."

"If your fields prosper, do not boast to your NEIGHBOR; there is great respect for the silent person. A person of character is a person of wealth. It is the lonely person whom God nurtures while the family man prays for a follower."

"You shalt never forget what thy mother has done for thee, she bares thee and nourished thee in all manner of ways. If you forget her, she might blame thee, she might lift up her arms to God, and God would hear her complaint. After the appointed months she bare thee, she nursed thee for three years. She brought thee up, and when you did enter the school, and was instructed in the writings, she came daily to thy master with bread and beer from her house."

"Never forget to be respectful, and do not sit down while another stands, who is older than you, or who holds a higher office than you does."

"Be not importunate nor indiscreet; enter not uninvited into the house of another; if he bids thee enter, you art honored. Look not around, in the house of another. If thine eye see anything, be silent about it, and relate it not outside to others, lest if it be heard, it become to thee as a crime worthy of death."

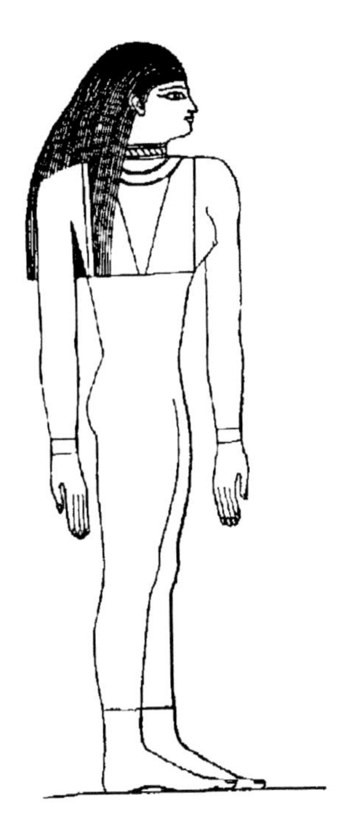

"Knowledge without action is like hoarding precious metals, a vain and foolish thing. Knowledge is like wealth, intended for use; Those who violate the universal law of USE conflict with natural forces."

"If you are poor, serve a good person so that your conduct will be well with God. Do not mention the fact that they were once poor or feel arrogant or resentful about it. Respect them for their position of authority, since fortune has its own laws; it is God's gift. God protects them or may turn away from them."

"If you are wise, train children to be pleasing to God. If they are straight and take after you, take good care of them. Do everything that is good for them. They are your children, your KA begot them. Don't withdraw your heart from them. But an offspring can make trouble. If they stray and neglect your council and disobey all that is said, with mouth spouting evil speech, then punish them for all their talk. God will hate them who cross you. Their guilt was determined in the womb. Those who God makes boatless cannot cross the water."

"If you are a guard, stand at your post even if you are fatigued. Keen is the face to him who enters announced, and spacious is the seat of they who have been asked to come in. Only a God can penetrate the secure place where rules are followed, even by privileged persons."

"If you are in authority, then you should do perfect things, those which will be remembered by posterity. Never listen to the words of flatterers or words that fill you with pride and vanity."

"If you are a judge, don't stop a person from telling you everything they want to tell you. A person in distress wants to pour out their heart even more than they want their case to be won. If you stop the person who is pleading, that person will say "why does this judge reject my plea?" Of course, not all that one pleads can be granted, but a good hearing soothes the heart. The means for getting a true and clear explanation is to listen with kindness."

"The God will judge the right."

"If you want friendship to endure in the house that you enter, the house of a master, of a brother or a friend, then in whatever place you enter beware of approaching the women there. Unhappy is the place where this is done. Unwelcome is he who intrudes on them. A thousand men are turned away from their good because of a short moment that is like a dream, and then that moment is followed by death that comes from having known that dream. Anyone who encourages you to take advantage of the situation gives you poor advice. When you go to do it your heart says no. If you are one who fails through the lust of women, then no affair of yours can prosper."

EGYPTIAN PROVERBS

ON LISTENING

"The lips of Wisdom are closed, Except to the ears of Understanding."

Give your ears, hear the sayings,
Give your heart to understand them;
It is an advantage to put them in your heart,
If you neglect them you will suffer!
Let them rest in the container of your belly,
May they be bolted in your heart;
(2) When there rises a whirlwind of words,
They'll be a mooring post for your tongue, a guide.
If you make your life with these in your heart, You will find it success and safety;
You will find my words a storehouse for life; Your being will prosper while upon earth.

"They who hear are beloved of GOD. Hearing creates good will. Hearing the voice of FATHER-MOTHER GOD requires silence of the body and of the mind."

"Hear the words of prudence, give heed unto her counsels, and store them in thine heart; her maxims are universal, and all the virtues lean upon her; she is the guide and the mistress of human life."

ON FORGIVENESS

"If you are angered by a misdeed, then lean toward a man on account of his rightness. Pass over the misdeed and don't remember it, since GOD was silent to you on the first day of your misdeed."

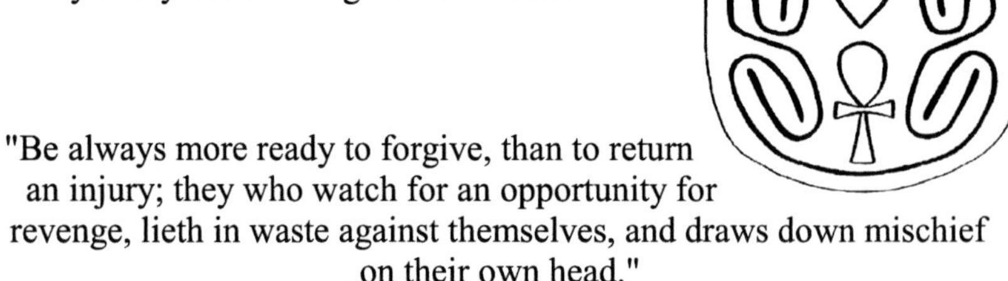

"Why do you seek revenge, O man! With what purpose is it that you pursue it? Do you think you to pain thine adversary by it? Know that you thyself feel its greatest torments."

"Be always more ready to forgive, than to return an injury; they who watch for an opportunity for revenge, lieth in waste against themselves, and draws down mischief on their own head."

"The root of revenge is in the weakness of the Soul; the most abject and timorous are the most addicted to it."

"One cannot force another to grow beyond their capacity."

ON NON-VIOLENCE

"If you meet a disputant who is more powerful than you, fold your arms and bend your back. Confrontation will not make them agree with you. Disregard their evil speech. Your self control will match their evil utterances and people will call them ignoramuses."

For it is evil to destroy,
Difficult to restore what one has damaged,
To rebuild what one has demolished.
Beware of it! An action is repaid by its like,
And to every action there is a consequence (response-opposite reaction).

EGYPTIAN PROVERBS

ON CHANGE

"Change is Lord of the Universe."

"Nothing rests, everything moves; everything vibrates."

READINESS TO GROW SPIRITUALLY

"When the ears of the student are ready to hear, then come the lips to fill them with wisdom."

"When the student is ready, the master will appear."

"Those who understand or believe will be persecuted and ridiculed."

"The lips of the wise are as the doors of a cabinet; no sooner are they opened, but treasures are poured out before you. Like unto trees of gold arranged in beds of silver, are wise sentences uttered in due season."

DOUBLE NATURE OF THE HUMAN BEING

"Humankind is the sole animal that is twofold. One part is simple: the human "essential", as say the Greeks, but which we call "the form of the divine similitude". Humankind is also fourfold: that which the Greeks call "hylic", which we call "cosmic."

"Twain are the forms of food-for soul and body, of which all animals consist... Some are nourished with the twofold form, while others with a single... Their soul is nourished by the ever-restless motion of the Cosmos; their bodies have their growth from foods drawn up from the water and the earth of the inferior world."

"GOD hath made Humankind of soul and body-that is, of an eternal and a mortal nature; so that an animal thus blended can content the dual origin-admire and worship things in heaven, and cultivate and govern things on earth... For it is plain that Humankind could not have sustained the strain of both, unless formed out of both natures, so as to be able to possess the powers of cultivating earthly things and loving Heaven."

"Something is added to thee unlike to what you seest; something animates thy clay higher than all that is the object of thy senses. Behold, what is it? Thy body remaineth perfect matter after IT is fled, therefore IT is no part of it; IT is immaterial, therefore IT is accountable for its actions."

EGYPTIAN PROVERBS

ON BALANCE AND HARMONY

"Harmony is the union of opposites."

"In all thy undertaking, let a reasonable assurance animate thy endeavors; if you despair of success, you shalt not succeed."

"Set your goodness before people,
Then you are greeted by all"

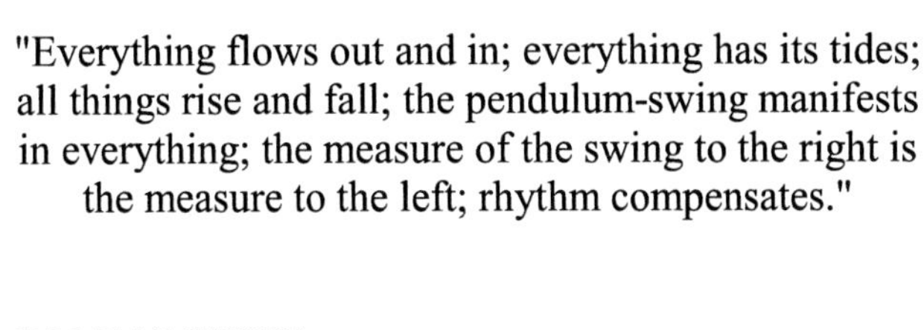

"Everything flows out and in; everything has its tides; all things rise and fall; the pendulum-swing manifests in everything; the measure of the swing to the right is the measure to the left; rhythm compensates."

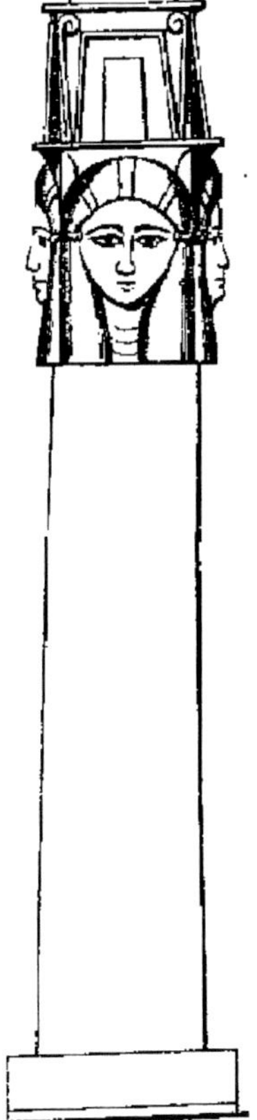

ON TALKING

"Speak not too much, for men are deaf to the man of many words; be silent rather, then shalt you please, therefore speak not. Before all things guard thy speech, for a man's ruin lies in his tongue. The body is a storehouse, full of all manner of answers. Choose therefore the right one and speak well, and let the wrong answer remain imprisoned in thy body."

"Maligning others is abhorred by the KA."

"Words cannot give wisdom if they stray from the truth."

"Don't repeat slander nor should you even listen to it. It is the spouting of the hot bellied. Just report a thing that has been observed, not something that has been heard secondhand. If it is something negligible, don't even say anything. He who is standing before you will recognize your worth."

"If you are among the people, gain your supporters by building trust. The trusted are those who do not speak the first thing to come to mind; and they will become leaders. If people of means have a good name, and their face is benign, people will praise them even without their knowledge. Those whose hearts obey their bellies, however, ask for contempt instead of love. Their hearts are naked. Their bodies are unanointed. The great hearted are a gift from God. Those who are ruled by their appetites belong to the enemy."

"Proceed not to speak or to act before you hast weighed thy words, and examined the tendency of every step you shalt take; so shall disgrace fly far from you, and in thy house shall shame be a stranger; repentance shall not visit you, nor sorrow dwell upon thy cheek in this or many lives to come."

"Put a bridle on thy tongue; set a guard before thy lips, lest the words of thine own mouth destroy thy peace...On much speaking cometh repentance, but in silence is safety."

OPPOSITES IN CREATION

"Man is separated into Soul and Body, and only when the two sides of his senses agree together, does utterance of its thought conceived by mind take place."

"Gender is in everything; everything has its Masculine and Feminine Principles; Gender manifests on all planes."

"Evil as well as good, both operate to advance the Great Plan."

"To have peace there must be strife; both are part of the structure of the world and requirements for the instruction of the children of GOD."

"Everything is dual; everything has poles; everything has its pair of opposites; like and unlike are the same; opposites are identical in nature, but different in degree; extremes meet; all truths are but half-truths; all paradoxes may be reconciled."

"Doth not the sun harden the clay? Doth it not also soften the wax? As is one sun that worketh both, even so it is one Soul that willeth contrarieties."

ON WILL AND RESOLUTION

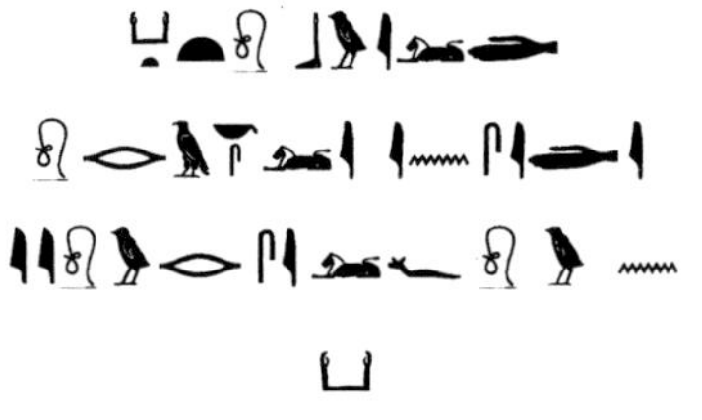

"Beware of irresolution in the intent of thy actions, beware of instability in the execution; so shalt you triumph over two great failings of thy nature."

"Complacency, regret and sorrow are the discouragers from evil; know that ye are Gods with a divine destiny, discouragers are transient distractions leading away from the path of light."

"Be you incapable of change in that which is right, and men will rely upon you. Establish unto thyself principles of action; and see that you ever act according to them. First know that thy principles are just, and then be you inflexible in the path of them."

"Those who gave you a body, furnished it with weakness; but The ALL who gave you Soul, armed you with resolution. Employ it, and you art wise; be wise and you art happy."

"The greatest bounties given to us are, judgment and will; happy are they who misapply them not."

DIVINE NATURE OF MAN AND WOMAN

"Gods are immortal men, and men are mortal Gods."

"Something is added to you unlike to what you see; something animates thy clay higher than all that is the object of thy senses. Behold, what is it? Thy body remains STILL matter after IT is fled, therefore IT is no part of it; IT is immaterial, therefore IT is accountable for its actions."

ON TEACHING AND LEARNING

"Everything is a teacher."

"The self chooses the proper instruction for self."

"To teach one must know the student; to know the student one must know the student's symbolism."

"I am the Mind - the Eternal Teacher. I am the begetter of the Word - the Redeemer of all humankind - and in the nature of the wise, the Word takes flesh. By means of the Word, the world is saved. I, Thought - the begetter of the Word, the Mind - come only unto they that are holy, good, pure and merciful, and that live piously and religiously, and my presence is an inspiration and a help to them, for when I come, they immediately know all things and adore the Universal Spirit. Before such wise and philosophic ones die, they learn to renounce their senses, knowing that these are the enemies of their immortal Souls."

"They who grasps the truth of the Mental Nature of the Universe are well advanced on The Path to Self Mastery."

"Because the Begetter of all things consists of Life and Light, whereof Humankind is made. If, therefore, a Human shall learn and understand the nature of Life and Light, then shall the Human pass into the eternity of Life and Light."

One will do all you say
If you are versed in writings;
Study the writings; put them in your heart,
Then all your words will be effective.

"Learn that the advantage lieth not in possessing good things but in knowing the use of them."

"Strive to see with the inner eye, the heart. It sees the reality not subject to emotional or personal error; it sees the essence. Intuition then is the most important quality to develop."
"Never forget: the words are not the reality, only reality is reality; picture symbols are the idea, words are confusion."

"Teach the great what is useful to them. Be an aide before the great to the people. If you let your knowledge impress your leader, your subsistence from them will come from their Soul. As their favorite's belly is filled, so will your back be clothed and their help will be there to sustain you. For your leader whom you love and who lives by useful knowledge, they in turn will give you good support. Thus will the love of you endure in his belly. They are Souls who love to listen."

EGYPTIAN PROVERBS

"Every gesture, is a world to be mastered."

"If an example is set by him or her who leads, he or she will be beneficent forever, their wisdom lasting for all time."

"Increase ye in increasing, and multiply in multitude, ye creatures and creations all; and man that hath Mind in him, let him learn to know that he himself is deathless, and that the cause of death is love, though love is all."

"Beware of falsehoods from misunderstood teachings."
"The study of nature is the first rung on the ladder to greater understanding."

"Disregarding the absurd or unorthodox may mean a lost chance to understand the universal laws."

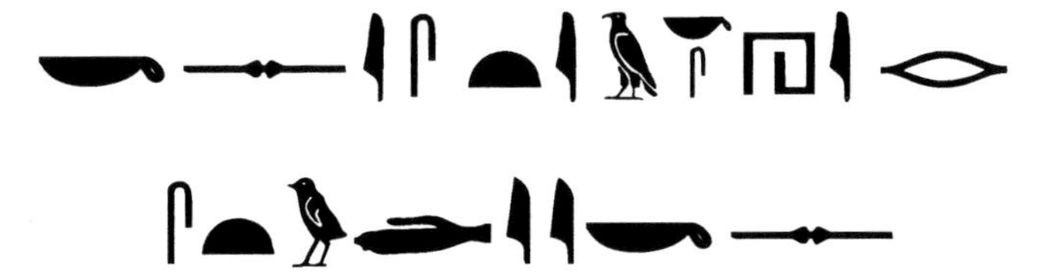

"The Cosmos is like a book, anyone who learns the language can read the knowledge and history of humanity."

" If your child accepts your words then no plan of theirs will go wrong. So teach your son to be a hearer, one who will be valued by the officials, one who will guide their speech by what they have been told, one who is regarded as a hearer. The children will reach old age if they listen to the wise words of their parents."

"Every parent teaches as they act. They will speak to the children so that they will speak to their children. They will set an example and not give offense."

ON INSULT AND INJURY

"As the tempest and the thunder affect not the sun or the stars, but spend their fury on stones and trees below; so injuries ascend not to the Soul of the great, but waste themselves on such as those who offer them.

ON SACRIFICE

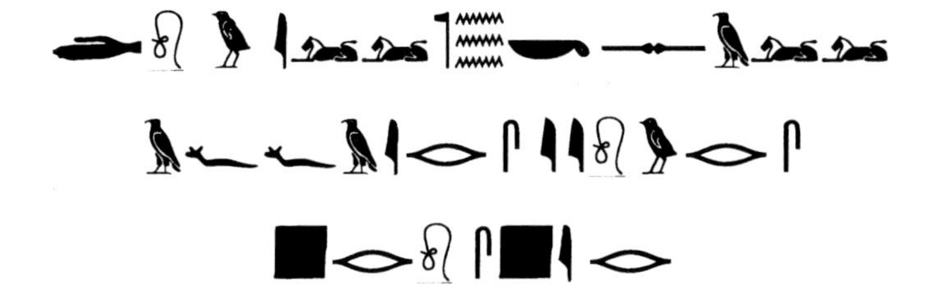

"Sacrifice protects the spirit from the pursuit of physical gratification."

"Sacrifice the first portions of the harvest, that your strength and faith to bring about what you desire may be increased; give the FIRST portion, to avoid danger of worldly indulgence; Give that you may receive. Fulfill the requirements of the universal law of equilibrium"

ON TRANSCENDING THE EGO

"Self sacrifice annihilates the personality."

"On the journey to the truth, one must stay on the path of love and enlightenment, the heart filled with greed and lust will be overcome by its selfishness."

ON TEMPTATION AND THE ILLUSION OF YOUTH AND COMPLEMENTS

"In the spring of thy youth, in the morning of thy days, when the eyes of others gaze on thee with delight, and nature whispers in thine ear the meaning of their looks; Ah! hear with caution their seducing words, guard well thy heart, nor listen to their soft persuasion."

"The messenger comes to thee...even as the old...say not to him: I am young...death comes and takes as first offering the child from the mother's breast as well as the man who has grown old."

EGYPTIAN PROVERBS

ON SIMPLICITY

"The nature of the body is to take delight and pleasure in complexity; the way of truth is that of simplicity."

"Complexity is the decadence of society; simplicity is the path of reality and salvation."

ON PAST LIVES

"The Race is never taught, but when God willeth it, its memory is restored by the Creator. You will see within yourself the Simple Vision brought to Birth by the compassion of God; no one can be saved before Rebirth."

ON KNOWLEDGE

"They know themselves; they know the Cosmos as well."

"To God, Knowledge is no beginning; rather Knowledge doth afford to us the first beginning of It's being known."

"True knowledge comes from the upward path which leads to the eternal Fire; error, defeat and death result from following the lower path of worldly attachment."

"He Whose face is half Black and half Gold can lead you upward"

ON DISHONESTY

"Do not conspire against others. GOD will punish accordingly. Schemes do not prevail; only the laws of GOD do. Live in peace, since what GOD gives comes by itself."

ON HONESTY

"The blessings of thy eternal part are health, vigor, and proportion. The greatest of these is health. What health is to the body, even that is honesty to the Soul."

"If you examine the character of a friend, don't ask other people, approach your friend. Deal with them alone, so as not to suffer from their anger. You may argue with them after a little while. You may test their heart in conversation. If what they have seen escapes them, if they do something that annoys you, stay friendly with them and do not attack. Be restrained and don't answer them with hostility. Do not leave them and do not attack them. Their time will not fail to come. They cannot escape their fate."

ON ARGUMENT AND CONFUSION

"They who know self, good and pious are, and still while on earth, divine. They will not say much nor lend their ear to much. For those who spend time in arguing and hearing arguments, doth shadow fight. God is not to be obtained by speech or hearing."

"The Greek tongue is a noise of words, a language of argument and confusion."

"One who is argumentative is a mildless person. If they are also known as an aggressor, then that hostile person will have trouble in the neighborhood."

From: The Instruction to Merikare.

" LO THE MISERABLE ASIATIC"

DURING the ninth dynasty, 3000 B.C.E., before the first Eurasian invasion of Egypt by the Hyksos, a Pharaoh passed on to his heir the following wisdom:

"Lo the miserable Asiatic, he is wretched because of the place he's in, short of water, bare of wood. Its paths are many and painful because of mountains. He does not dwell in one place. Food propels his legs. He fights since the time of Horus."

ON GOOD NATUREDNESS

"Know your friends and then you prosper. Don't be mean to your friends. They are like a watered field and greater than any material riches that you may have, for what belongs to one belongs to another. The character of one who is well born should be a profit to him. Good nature is a memorial."

ON DRUGS

"Oh that you did understand that wine is an abomination."

"Drink not beer to excess! The words that come out of thy mouth, you can not recall. You does fall and break thy limbs, and no one reaches out to thee. Thy comrades go on drinking, they stand up and say: 'Away with this fellow who is drunk.' If any one should seek thee to ask counsel of thee, you would be found lying in the dust like a little child."

ON HATRED, ENVY, HYPOCRISY, DECEIT, AMBITION

"The heart of the envious is gall and bitterness; his tongue spits venom; the success of his neighbor breaks his rest. He sits in his cell repining; and the good that happens to another, is to him an evil. Hatred and malice feed upon his heart, and there is no rest in him."

"An envious person wax lean with the fatness of their neighbors. Envy is the daughter of pride, the author of murder, the beginner of secret sedition, and the perpetual tormentor of virtue. Envy is the filthy slime of the soul; a venom, a poison, or quicksilver which consumes the flesh, and dries up the marrow of the bones."

"Attribute not the good actions of others to bad causes: you cannot know their heart; but the world will know by this that thine is full of envy."

EGYPTIAN PROVERBS

"The heart of the hypocrite is hid in his breast; he masks his words in the semblance of truth, while the business of his life is only to deceive."

"The ambitious will always be first in the crowd; pressing forward, looking not behind. More anguish is it to their mind to see one before them, than joy to leave thousands at a distance."

Conquer malice in your self,
A quarrelsome man does not rest on the morrow.
Keep away from a hostile man,
Do not let him be your comrade;
Befriend one, who is straight and true,
One whose actions you have seen.
If your rightness matches his,
The friendship will be balanced.

Do not enter into a crowd,
If you find it in an uproar
And about to come to blows.
Don't pass anywhere near by,
Keep away from their tumult,
Lest you be brought before the court,
When an inquiry is made.
Stay away from hostile people,
Keep your heart quiet among fighters;
An outsider is not brought to court,
One who knows nothing is not bound in fetters.

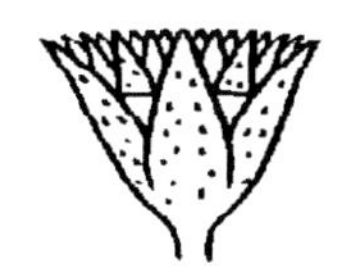

ON REVENGE

"Think not you art revenged of thine enemies when you slay them; you put them beyond thy reach, you give them quiet, and take from thyself all means of hurting them."

"There is nothing so easy as to revenge an offence; but nothing is so honorable as to pardon it."

They [the unrighteous liars, schemers, etc] are rich in grief through the might of God.

ON CONTENTMENT

"To be satisfied with little is the greatest wisdom; and they that increase their riches, increase their cares; but a contented mind is a hidden treasure, and trouble find it not."

"An immoderate desire of riches is a poison lodged in the mind. It contaminates and destroys everything that was good in it. It is no sooner rooted there, than all virtue, all honesty, all natural affection, fly before the face of it."

ON THE ILLUSION BORNE FROM THE HUMAN SENSES

"The senses give the meaning from a worldly point of view; see with the spirit and the true meaning will be revealed. This is the relationship between the object and its Creator, its true meaning."

EGYPTIAN PROVERBS

"Knowledge derived from the senses is illusory, true knowledge can only come from the understanding of the union of opposites."

"The delusion is believing that there are disunions. All things are one."

"In the study of causes, be on guard against illusion, lest you confuse the primal source cause with mere effect."

"Be not fooled, magic cannot alter the laws of nature, all must be according to Law; but an adept can, through control of thought and Law, alter the perception of the spectators since the senses bring information not knowledge."

"It is very hard, to leave the things we have grown used to, which meet our gaze on every side. Appearances delight us, whereas things which appear not, make their believing hard. Evils are the more apparent things, whereas the Good can never show Itself unto the eyes, for It hath neither form nor figure."

ON WISDOM

"The many do confound philosophy with multifarious reasoning... by mixing it, by means of subtle expositions, with diverse sciences not easy to be grasped-such as arithmetic, and music, and geometry. But pure philosophy, which doth depend on Godly piety alone, should only so far occupy itself with other arts, that it may appreciate the working out in numbers of the fore-appointed stations of the stars when they return, and of the course of their procession...know how to appreciate the Earth's dimensions, qualities and quantities, the Water's depths, the strength of Fire, and the effect and nature of all these... give worship and give praise unto the Art and Mind of God."

"Wisdom is a child of training; Truth is the child of Wisdom and Love."

"Death comes when the purpose of living is fulfilled; death shows what the reason for living was."

"Scorn also to depress thy competitor by any dishonest or unworthy method; strive to raise thyself above them by excelling them; so shall thy contest for superiority to be crowned with honor, if not with success."

"If the social order judges success by material gain, the most successful will be the most corruptible and selfish."

"Accurate reckoning (mathematics), the entrance into the knowledge of all existing things and all obscure secrets."

"If you meet a disputant who is not your equal or match, do not attack, they are weak. They will confound themselves. Do not answer the evil speech and give in to your animal passion for combat by venting your self against them. You will beat them through the reproof of the witnesses who will agree with you."

"What is the pay for titles, but flattery? How does man purchase power but by being a slave to him who giveth it?"

"Magic is knowledge and strength; without strength, nothing worthwhile can be achieved, without knowledge, strength is uncontrolled."

"As above, so below; as below, so above."

"The mover must have greater power than the moved."

"All that exists on earth is an incarnation of the real essence from the non-material realm."

"Courage, will, knowledge and silence are essential qualities for those on the path of perfection."

"They who began to benefit from words of wisdom while they were children shall prosper in their affairs."

ON CONTROLLING THE EMOTIONS AND SENSES

"By keeping in subjection the belly, you wilt be listened to. If you have eaten three loaves of bread, and have drunk two vessels of beer, if you are not full contend against greediness."

"If you want to have perfect conduct, to be free from evil, then above all guard against the vice of greed. Greed is a grievous sickness that has no cure. There is no treatment for it. It embroils fathers, mothers and the brothers of the mother. It parts the wife from the husband. Greed is a compound of all the evils; a bundle of all hateful things.

line, for that person will leave a legacy by such behavior. On the other hand, the greedy has no tomb."

"Do not be greedy in the division of things. Do not covet more than your share. Don't be greedy toward your relatives. A mild person has a greater claim than a harsh one. Poor is the person who forgets their relatives; they are deprived of their company. Even a little bit of what is wanted will turn a quarreler into a friendly person."

"Do not be greedy and you'll find profit."

"Things subject to birth abound in passions, birth in itself being passable. But where there's passion, nowhere is there Good; and where is Good, nowhere a single passion. For where is day, nowhere is night; and where is night, day is nowhere."

"When emotions are societies objective, tyranny will govern regardless of the ruling class."

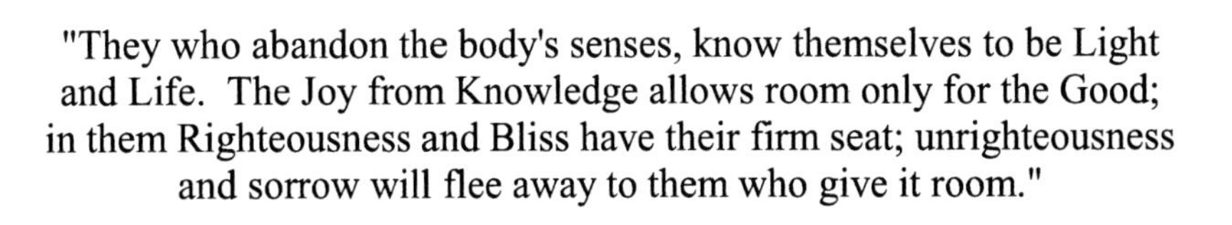

"They who abandon the body's senses, know themselves to be Light and Life. The Joy from Knowledge allows room only for the Good; in them Righteousness and Bliss have their firm seat; unrighteousness and sorrow will flee away to them who give it room."

" Conceal your heart, control your mouth. Beware of releasing the restraints in you; Listen if you want to endure in the mouth of the hearers. Speak after you have mastered the craft."

"When you answer one who is fuming, turn your face and control yourself. The flame of the hot hearted sweeps across everything. But those who step gently, their path is a paved road. Those who are agitated all day have no happy moments, but those who amuse themselves all day can't keep their fortune."

"As the whirlwind in its fury tares up trees, and deforms the face of nature, or as an earthquake in its convulsions overturns whole cities, so the rage of an angry person throws mischief around them."

"Associate not with a passionate man, nor approach him in conversations; Leap not to cling to such a one, that the terror carry you not away."

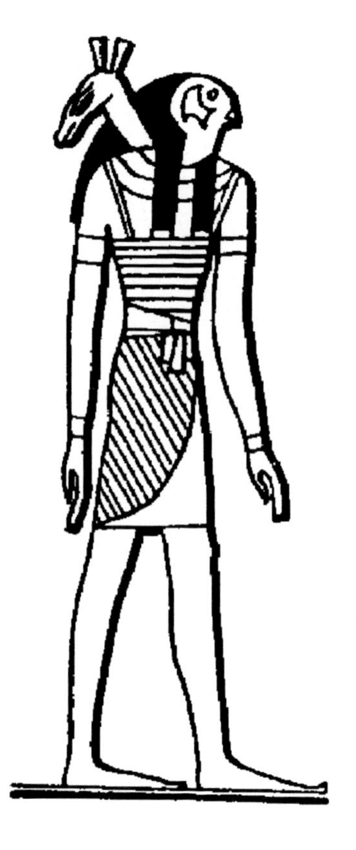

"Indulge not thyself in the passion of Anger; it is whetting a sword to wound thine own breast, or murder thy friend."

"Passions and irrational desires are ills exceedingly great; and over these GOD hath set up the Mind to play the part of judge and executioner."

"Feelings are good servants but poor masters."

"The worst things: To be in bed and sleep not, To want for one who comes not, To try to please and please not."

"When ye have served your time, and have put off the world's restraint, and freed yourselves from deathly bonds, pray that GOD may restore you pure and holy to the nature of your higher self, that is of the Divine! Those who have lived in other fashion - impiously - both is return to Heaven denied, and there's appointed them migration into other bodies unworthy of a holy soul and base...souls in their life on earth run risk of losing hope of future immortality."

"There are two roads traveled by humankind, those who seek to live MAAT and those who seek to satisfy their animal passions."

"Mastery of the passions, allows divine thought and action."

"Associate not with a passionate man; Nor approach him in conversations; Leap not to cleave to such a one, That the terror carry thee not away."

"An infant's Soul is altogether a thing of beauty to see, not yet befouled by body's passions, still all but hanging from the Cosmic Soul! But when the body grows in bulk and draws down the Soul into its mass, then does the Soul cut off itself and bring upon itself forgetfulness, and no more shares in the Beautiful and Good (God); and this forgetfulness becomes vice."

"If a Soul on entering in the human body persists in its vice, it neither tastes deathlessness nor share in the Good; but speeding back again it turns into the path that leads to creeping things. This is the sentence of the vicious soul."

"The Soul that hath no knowledge of the things that are or knowledge of their nature, is blinded by the body's passions and tossed about. The wretched Soul, not knowing what it is, becomes the slave of bodies of strange form in sorry plight, bearing the body as a load; not as the ruler but as the ruled."

"I, GOD, am present with the holy and good, those who are pure and merciful, who live piously and give up their body unto its proper death. To them, my presence becomes an aid, straight-away they gain inner vision, knowledge of all things, and win the my love by their pure lives, and give thanks, invoking the my blessings and chanting hymns, intent on the me with ardent love. It is I, who will not let the operations that befall the body work to their natural end. I'll close all the entrances, and cut the mental actions off which base and evil energies induce. Mind-less ones, the wicked and depraved, the envious and covetous, and those who murder or do and love impiety, I am far off, yielding my place to the Avenging Demon, who rush on them through their senses."

"It is not possible to give one's Self to the body and the bodiless, things perishable and things divine. The one who has the will to choose is left the choice of one or other; for it can never be the two should meet. And in those Souls to whom the choice is left, the waning of the one causes the other's growth to show itself."

"Do not speak words of pride, even when you art sitting with thyself."

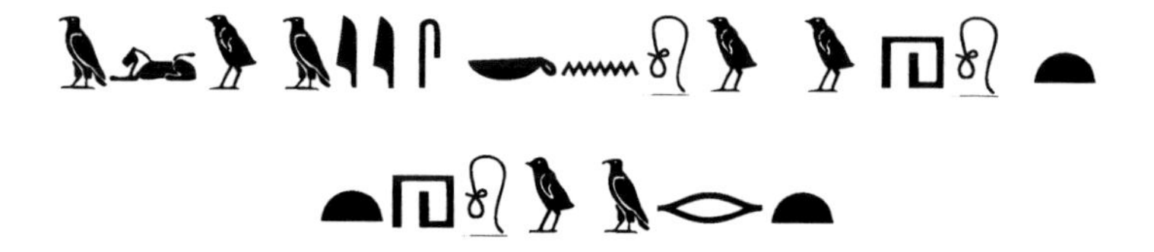

"Do not be proud and arrogant with your knowledge. Consult with the ignorant and wise. Truth may be found among maids at the grindstones."

EGYPTIAN PROVERBS

"Vain and inconstant if you art, how can you but be weak? Is not inconstancy connected with frailty? Avoid the danger of the one, and you shall escape the mischief of the other."

"Before such wise and philosophic ones die, they learn to renounce their senses, knowing that these are the enemies of their immortal Souls."

"To free the spirit, control the senses; the reward will be a clear insight."

"Something is added to you unlike to what you see; something animates thy clay higher than all that is the object of thy senses. Behold, what is it? Thy body remains STILL matter after IT is fled, therefore IT is no part of it; IT is immaterial, therefore IT is accountable for its actions."

ON EVIL

"By the Maker's self naught is there thought or bad or base. These things are passions which accompany the making process, as rust does brass and filth does the body; but neither does the brass-smith make rust, nor the begetters of the body filth, nor God manufacture evil."

"They say that God ought to have freed the World from bad in every way...this was foreseen by Highest God, endowing the minds of men and women with sense and intelligence. For it is by these things alone whereby we stand above the rest of animals, that we are able to avoid the snares and crimes of ill. For those who shall on sight have turned from them, before he hath become immersed in them - they are protected by divine intelligence and divine prudence."

"I have made an end of my failings, I have removed my defects. What then is it? The separation of the corruptible matter, it is the initiate, triumphant before the Gods all. Driven away are all of the defects which belong to him. What is this then? This is the purification on the day of his new birth."

"Evil as well as good both operate to advance the Great Plan."

"Beautiful to God are the things which men think mean, since in truth they have been made to serve the laws of God."

"When the soul gets to know the creator of it's peace, it's filled with love, and forgetfulness of every ill, and can no more keep from the Good: truth and righteousness. Never can an embodied Soul that has gotten hold upon the truly good and True, slip back again into the contrary."

EGYPTIAN PROVERBS

ON STEADFASTNESS

"I am steadfast, son of steadfast, conceived and born in the region of steadfastness. "

ON FEAR

Do not lie down in fear of tomorrow:
"Comes day, how will tomorrow be?"
Man ignores how tomorrow will be;
God is ever in his perfection,
Man is ever in his failure.
"Truth protects from fear."

"The expectation and the fear of death torture the multitude, who do not know True Reason."

ON COMPLACENCY.

"Complacency, regret and sorrow are the discouragers from Set (evil); know that ye are Gods with a divine destiny; discouragers are but transient distractions leading away from the path of light."

ON LOVE AND JOY

"If you wish to be as a master you must love impersonally, caring for all equally; wants must yield to self control, live as though you have achieved and acquired everything you need and also as if you have lost everything; even the thing or person you might love most; for material things are transitory."

"Those who through the error of attachment love their body, abide wandering in darkness, sensible and suffering the things of death, but those who realize that the body is but the tomb of the Soul, rise to immortality."

ON SILENCE

"Be still and solemn silence keep; then shall GOD open the way for salvation. Withdraw into thyself and Father-Mother God will come. Throw away the work of the body's senses and thy divinity will come to birth; purge from thyself the animal torments, concerns with things of matter."

"The abomination of the sanctuary of GOD is: too much talking. Pray you with a loving heart the petitions of which all are in secret. GOD will do thy business, hear that which you say and will accept thine offerings."

"If you meet a disputant who is your equal, you will overcome them with silence while they speak evilly. Those who witness the encounter will remark on this and your name will be held in high esteem among the great."

EGYPTIAN PROVERBS

"Those who knoweth GOD, being filled with all good things, think Godly thoughts and not thoughts like the many think; For this cause, they who Gnostic are, please not the many, nor the many them. They are thought mad and laughed at; they are hated and despised, and sometimes even put to death."

"It is better either to be silent, or to say things of more value than silence. Sooner throw a pearl at hazard than an idle or useless word; and do not say a little in many words, but a great deal in few."

"If you are a man of worth who sits at the council of a leader, concentrate on being excellent. Your silence is much better than boasting. Speak when you know that you have a solution. It is the skilled person who should speak when in council. Speaking is harder than all other work. The one who understands this makes speech a servant."

"Knowing the Good is Holy Silence. For neither can who perceive It, perceive anything else; nor gaze on aught else; nor hear aught else; nor stir the body in any way. And shining then all around the mind, It shines through the whole soul, and draws it out of body, transforming all of you to essence. For it is possible, that the soul should be made like to God, even while it still is in a body, if it does contemplate the Beauty of the Good."

ON WRONG THINKING

"Searching for one's self in the world is the pursuit of an illusion."

"As you think so shall you become."

"Virtues fail that are frustrated by passion at every turn."

"As a rock on the sea shore, stand firm, and let not the dashing of the waves disturb you. Raise your head like a tower on a hill, and the arrows of fortune drop at your feet. In the instant of danger, the courage of your heart will sustain you, and the steadiness of your mind beareth you through."

"The extension of the intellect which we possess for the survey of transcendent things, is very narrow; but most ample when it shall perceive with the felicity of self-consciousness."

"The all is mind; The Universe is Mental."

"Mind, as matter, may be transmuted, from state to state, degree to degree, condition to condition, pole to pole, vibration to vibration. Transmutation is a Mental Art."

EGYPTIAN PROVERBS

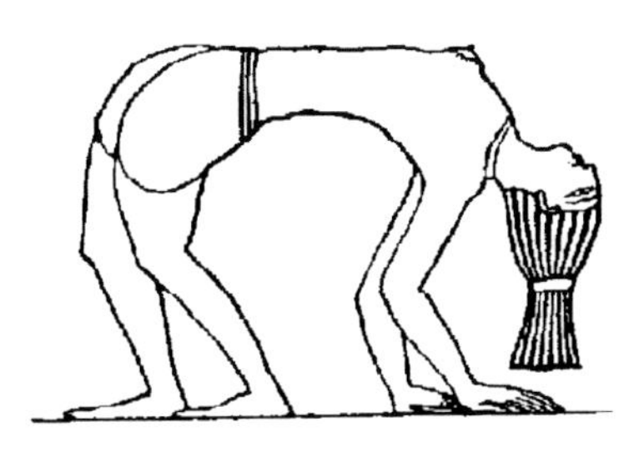

"It takes a strong disciple to rule over the mountainous thoughts and constantly go to the essence of the meaning; as mental complexity increases, thus will the depth of your decadence and challenge both be revealed."

"The secrets of the universe cannot be discovered through study and research alone but the honest search for truth and the development of a incorruptible mind qualifies the seeker for higher instruction."

"In the test of loneliness you have no one and nothing to fear but yourself!"

ON HEALTH

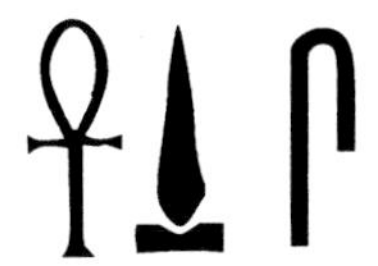

"The body becomes what the foods are, as the spirit becomes what the thoughts are."

"If you would preserve understanding and health to old age, avoid the allurements of Voluptuousness, and fly from its temptations.... For if you hearken unto the words of the Adversary, you art deceived and betrayed. The joy which it promises changes to madness, and its enjoyments lead on to diseases and death."

EGYPTIAN PROVERBS

"The blessings of thy eternal part, are health, vigor, and proportion. The greatest of these is health. What health is to the body, even that is honesty to the Soul. Develop your spirit that it may gain strength to control the body and follow the natural Laws of nutrition and hygiene."

"Her name is Health: she is the daughter of Exercise, who begot her on Temperance. The rose blushes on her cheeks, the sweetness of the morning breathes from her lips; joy, tempered with innocence and modesty, sparkles in her eyes and from the cheerfulness of her heart she sings as she walks."

"Yield not to emotion, for there are discarnate forces around us who desire emotional existence. In the heat of passion one surrenders to the influence of these, ill health and unwise living results. Through firm instruction one can master one's emotions and these forces; in this, make them serve one. Thus the slave becomes the master."

"If you would live in harmony with yourself and the Earth you must follow the laws of the Earth. For your body is of the Earth; lest it lead your SOUL to the path of disease, death and reincarnation. The Neters (angels) of the divine will desert you, and those of evil will destroy your body and your spirit."

"The source of evil is in your body. Evil entices the body through temptation of its weakest virtue. There can be no divinity in the unclean temple where abomination rules."

EGYPTIAN PROVERBS

"The source of illness is the food you ingest; to purge the dreadful UKHEDU
which lurks in your bowels, for three consecutive days each month purge yourself with a cattle horn, its sharp end clipped off so as to create a small opening (for water to run through)."

EGYPTIAN PROVERBS ON CONTROLLING AND SUBLIMATING THE SEXUAL LIFE FORCE INTO SPIRITUAL AND PSYCHIC ENERGY

"Be circumspect in matters of sexual relations."

"Though all men suffer fated things, those led by reason (guided by the HIGHER INTELLECT), do not endure suffering with the rest; but since they've freed themselves from viciousness, not being bad, they do not suffer bad. Though having thought fornication or murder but not having committed these, the Mind-led man will suffer just as though he had committed fornication, and though he be no murderer, as though he had committed murder because there was will to commit these things."

ON PRAYER

"The house of God hates too much speaking. Pray then with a loving heart, who's petitions are all in secret. God will listen and do thy business, and will accept your offerings."

"In offering to God, take care against the things which are against God. Witness with your EYE, the plans of God. Devote yourself to adore God's name. It is God who gives souls to millions of forms and GOD MAGNIFIES WHOEVER MAGNIFIES GOD."

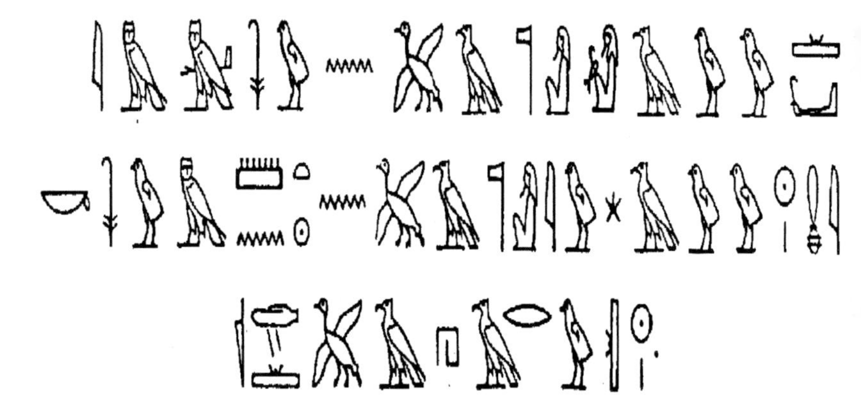

"If you raise your hands (adoration and prayer) to God, God will hear your prayer."

"Please the Gods so that they may not be angry with you, save the furthermost room of your house as a little chapel; In the sanctuary of the God - clamor is an abomination. Pray for thyself, with a loving heart, in which the words remain hidden; that God may supply thy need, hear thy words and accept thy offering."

"Pray that you may have the power to catch a thought of the mighty God, one single beam to shine into thy thinking; For thought alone "sees" the Unmanifest, in that it is itself unmanifest. All that is made manifest is subject to *becoming,* for it hath been *made* manifest. The Unmanifest forever is, for It does not desire to be made manifest, It for ever *is*, and makes manifest all other things."

DETACHMENT AND DISPASSION, WISDOM AND VIRTUE

"EMOTIONS ARE GOOD SERVANTS BUT POOR MASTERS".

"Truth has the force of emotion BEHIND it."

"Mastery of the passions allows divine thought and action."

"Virtues fail that are frustrated by passion at every turn."

"The body was created to be subservient to the Soul; while YOU afflict the Soul for the body's pain, behold YOU SET the body above it. As the wise afflict not their garment; so the patient grieve not their Soul because that which covers it is injured."

"Glory, like a shadow, flieth from they who pursue it; but it follows at the heels of they who would fly from it; if you courteth it without merit, you shall never attain unto it; if you deservest it, though you hidest thyself, it will never forsake you."

"Grief is natural to the mortal world, and is always about you; pleasure is a guest, and visiteth by thy invitation; use well thy mind, and sorrow shall be passed behind you; be prudent, and the visits of joy shall remain long with you."

EGYPTIAN PROVERBS

"Ambition is to spiritual development what termites are to wood."

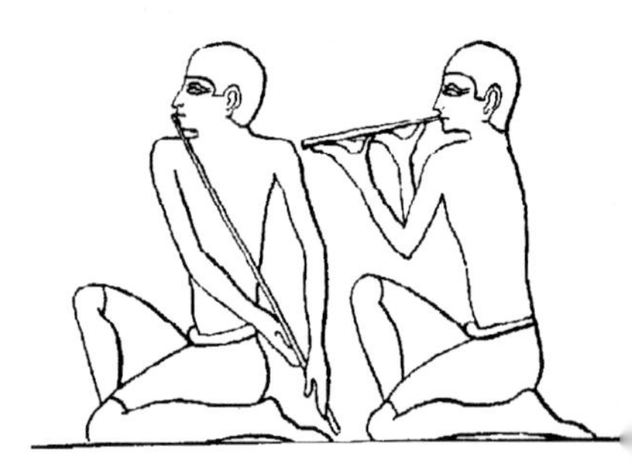

"Mind, as matter, may be transmuted from state to state, degree to degree, condition to condition, pole to pole and vibration to vibration. Transmutation is a Mental Art."

"He who grasps the truth of the Mental Nature of the Universe is well advanced on the Path to Self mastery."

"Purification of the Heart (consciousness) leads to the Highest Good: Eternal Life and Supreme Peace."

"Contemplate thy powers, contemplate thy wants and thy connections; so shall you discover the duties of life, and be directed in all thy ways."

"When an idea exclusively occupies the mind, it is transformed into an actual physical state."

"Reason of Divinity may not be known except by a concentration of the senses like onto it."

EGYPTIAN PROVERBS

"Wisdom that understands in silence; this is the matter and the womb from which humanity is born, and the True Good the seed."

"Get thyself ready and make the thought in you a stranger to the world-illusion."

"O praise the goodness of the Supreme Being with songs for thanksgiving, and meditate in silence on the wonders of HIS and HER love; let thy heart overflow with gratitude and acknowledgment, let the language of thy lips speak praise and adoration, let the actions of thy life show thy love to Universal Law."

"IF THOU WILT ATTENTIVELY DWELL (meditate) AND OBSERVE WITH THY HEART'S EYES, THOU WILL FIND THE PATH THAT LEADS ABOVE; NAY, THAT IMAGE SHALL BECOME THY GUIDE ITSELF, BECAUSE THE DIVINE SIGHT HATH THIS PECULIAR CHARM; IT HOLDETH FAST AND DRAWETH UNTO IT THOSE WHO SUCCEED IN OPENING THEIR EYES, JUST AS, THEY SAY, THE MAGNET THE IRON."

"Stand in a place uncovered to the sky, facing west to the sinking sun, and make your solemn worship, and the same way as he rises to the east in the morning. Now, make thy body still."

"You, alone can speak. Wonder at this glorious prerogative; and pay to the Supreme who gave to you the gift of life a rational and welcome praise, teaching your children wisdom, instructing the offspring of your loins in piety."

"Reflection is the business of Humankind; a sense of their state is the first duty: but who remembereth themselves in joy? Is it not in mercy then that sorrow is allotted unto us?"

EGYPTIAN PROVERBS

"Breath is life."

"I am the lotus pure coming forth from the god of light, the guardian of the nostril of Ra, the guardian of the nose of Hathor; I make my journey; I run after him who is Horus. I am the pure one coming forth from the fields."

Be Pure in the Horizon and do away with your impurities by bathing in the lake of Shu. (Shu is the god of air)

"Be as the Sun and Stars, that emanate the life giving essence; give life without asking for anything in return; to be a sun, breath rhythmically and deeply; then as RA shall you be."

"To change your mood or mental state, change your vibration."

"To destroy an undesirable rate of mental vibration, concentrate on the opposite vibration to the one to be suppressed."

"If you travel on a road made by your own hands each day, you will arrive at the place where you would want to be."

ADMONITIONS TO THE SPIRITUAL SEEKER

"On the journey to the truth, one must stay on the path of love and enlightenment, the heart filled with greed and lust will be overcome by its selfishness."

"Be not carried off by the fierce flood, but using the shore-current, ye who can, make for Salvation's port, and, harbouring there, seek ye for one to take ye by the hand and lead you unto the gates of self-knowledge."

"When the ears of the student are ready to hear, then come the lips to fill them with wisdom."

"The lips of Wisdom are closed, Except to the ears of Understanding."

"When the student is ready the master will appear."

"Those who understand or believe will be persecuted and ridiculed." "Of all marvels, that which most wins our wonder is that man has been able to find out the nature of the Gods and bring it into play. Since then, our earliest progenitors were in great error-seeing they had no rational faith about the Gods, and that they paid no heed unto their cult and holy worship-they chanced upon an art whereby they made Gods. To this invention they conjoined a power that suited it derived from cosmic nature; and blending these together, since souls they could not make, they evoked daimon's souls or those of angels; and attached them to their sacred images and holy mysteries, so that the statues should, by means of these, possess the powers of doing good and the reverse."

"Such words as these have few to give them ear; nay, probably they will not even have the few. They have , moreover, some strange force peculiar to themselves, for they provoke evil unto even more evil."

"And now that you have learnt these lessons, make promise to keep silence on thy virtue, and to no soul, make known the handling on to you the manner of Rebirth, that we may not be thought to be calumniators."

"Keep this teaching from translation in order that such mighty Mysteries might not come to the Greeks and to the disdainful speech of Greece, with all its looseness and its surface beauty, taking all the strength out of the solemn and the strong - the energetic speech of Names."

"Unto those who come across these words, their composition will seem most simple and clear; but on the contrary, as this is unclear, and has the true meaning of its words concealed, it will be still unclear, when, afterwards, the Greeks will want to turn our tongue into their own - for this will be a very great distorting and obscuring of even what has heretofore been written. Turned into our own native tongue, the teachings keepeth clear the meaning of the words. For that its very quality of sound, the very power of Egyptian names, have in themselves the bringing into act of what is said."

EGYPTIAN PROVERBS

"Avoid conversing with the many on your knowledge; not to keep it selfishly but to not seem ridiculous unto the multitude. The like's acceptable to the like; the unlike's never friend to the unlike."

"Let these words rest in the casket of thy belly, that they may act as a peg on thy tongue."

"The truth shall set you free."

"The spirit is life and the body is for living."

"Whosoever comprehends this work, grounded upon earth, like porcelain figures, at the hour of sunset, that is the triumph of Ra in Amenta over his enemies. For whosoever has knowledge upon earth, has knowledge after death."

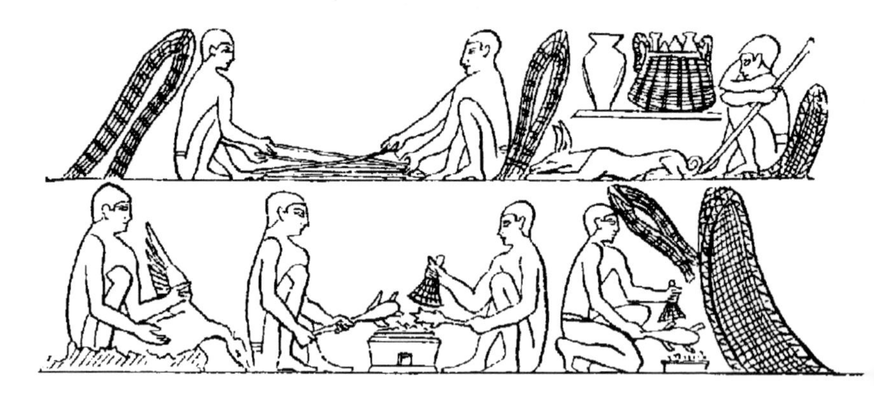

PART III
INTRODUCTION TO MEDITATION

TO THINK, TO PONDER, TO FIX ATTENTION, MEDITATION

EGYPTIAN MEDITATION TEACHINGS

"Contemplate thy powers, contemplate thy wants and thy connections; so shall you discover the duties of life, and be directed in all thy ways."

"When an idea exclusively occupies the mind, it is transformed into an actual physical state."

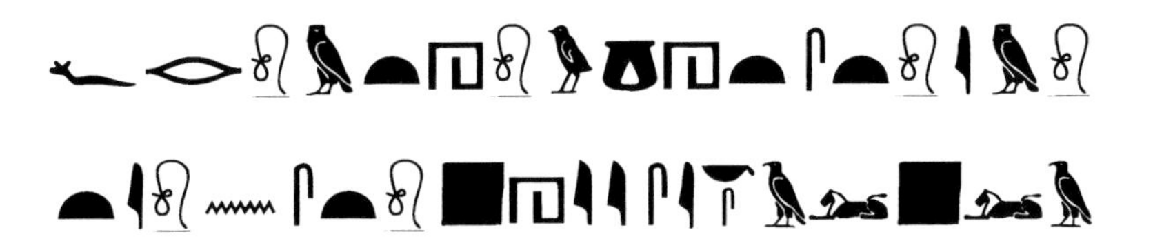

"Reason of Divinity may not be known except by a concentration of the senses like onto it."

"Wisdom that understands in silence, this is the matter and the womb from which humanity is born, and the True Good the seed."
"Get thyself ready and make the thought in you a stranger to the world-illusion."

"O praise the goodness of the Supreme Being with songs for thanksgiving, and meditate in silence on the wonders of HIS and HER love; let thy heart overflow with gratitude and acknowledgment, let the language of thy lips speak praise and adoration, let the actions of thy life show thy love to Universal Law."

"IF THOU WILT ATTENTIVELY DWELL (meditate) AND OBSERVE WITH THY HEART'S EYES, THOU'LT FIND THE PATH THAT LEADS ABOVE; NAY, THAT IMAGE SHALL BECOME THY GUIDE ITSELF, BECAUSE THE DIVINE SIGHT HATH THIS PECULIAR CHARM, IT HOLDETH FAST AND DRAWETH UNTO IT THOSE WHO SUCCEED IN OPENING THEIR EYES, JUST AS, THEY SAY, THE MAGNET THE IRON."

THE OLDEST KNOWN FORMAL MEDITATION:

The following instruction comes from the ancient Egyptian story of "The Destruction of Humankind":

"Whensoever Djehuti shall wish to recite this composition on behalf of Ra, he must perform a sevenfold purification for three days, and priests and ordinary men and women shall do likewise. Whosoever shall recite the above words shall perform the ceremonies which are to be performed when this book is being read. And they shall make their position in a circle which is beyond them, and their two eyes shall be fixed upon themselves, all their members shall be composed, [relaxed, motionless] and their steps shall not carry them away [from the place of meditation]. Whoever among men shall recite [these] words shall visualize themselves as Ra on the day of his birth; and his possessions shall not become fewer, and his house shall never fall into decay, but shall endure for a million eternities."

SIMPLE MEDITATION TECHNIQUE

Modern scientific research has proven that one of the most effective things anyone can do to promote mental and physical health is to sit quietly for 20 minutes twice each day. This is more effective than a change in diet, vitamins, food supplements, medicines, etc. It is not necessary to possess any special skill or training. All that is required is that one achieves a relaxed state of mind, unburdened by the duties of the day. You may sit from a few minutes up to an hour in the morning and in the late afternoon.

This simple practice, if followed each day, will promote above average physical health and spiritual evolution. One's mental and emotional health will be maintained in a healthy state as well. The most important thing to remember during this meditation time is to just relax and not try to stop the mind from pursuing a particular idea but also not trying to actively make the mind pursue a particular thought or idea. Sometimes one will know that one has been carried away into thoughts about what one needs to do, or who needs to be called, or is something burning in the kitchen?, etc. These thoughts are worldly thoughts. If a Hekau or Mantra (Prayer) is recited, or if a special hieroglyph is meditated upon, the mind should not be forced to hold it. Rather, one should direct the mind and when one realizes that one has been carried away with a particular thought, bring the mind gently back to the original object of meditation, in this way, it will eventually settle where it feels most comfortable and at peace.

With more practice, the awareness of the hekau or object of meditation (candle, mandala, etc.) will dissipate as you go deeper. This is the positive, meditative movement that is desired. The goal is to relax to such a degree that the mind drifts to deeper and deeper levels of consciousness, finally reaching the source of consciousness, the source of all thought; then the mind transcends even this level of consciousness and there, communes with the Absolute Reality, Neter Neteru. This is the state of "Cosmic Consciousness", the state of enlightenment. After a while, the mental process will remain at the Soul level all the time. This is the Enlightened Sage Level.

MEDITATION TIPS

Begin by meditating for 5 minutes each day, gradually building up the time. The key is consistency in time and place. Nature inspires us to establish a set routine to perform our activities; the sun rises in the east and sets in the west every day, the moon's cycle is every 28 days and the seasons change approximately at the same times of the year every year. It is better to practice for 5 minutes each day than 20 minutes one day and 0 minutes the next. Do a formal sit down meditation whenever the feeling comes to you but try to do it at least once a day. Do not eat for at least 2 hours before meditation. It is even more preferable to not eat 12 hours before. For example: eat nothing (except only water or tea) after 6 p.m. until after meditation at 6 a.m. the following morning. Do not meditate within 24 hours of having sexual intercourse. Meditate alone in a quiet area, in a dimly lit room (candle light is adequate). Do light exercise (example: Chi Kung or Hatha Yoga) before meditating, then say Hekau (affirmations, prayers, mantras, etc.) for a few minutes to set up positive vibrations in the mind. Burning your favorite incense is a good way to set the mood. Keep a ritualistic procedure about the meditation time. Do things in a slow, deliberate manner.

When ready, try to focus the mind on one object, symbol or idea such as the heart or Hetep (Supreme Peace). If the mind strays, bring it back gently. Patience, self-love and self-forgiveness are the keys here. Gradually, the mind will not drift toward thoughts or objects of the world. It will move toward subtler levels of consciousness until it reaches the source of the thoughts and there commune with that source, Neter Neteru. This is the desired positive movement of the practice of meditation because it is from Neter Neteru that all inspiration, creativity and altruistic feelings of love come. Neter Neteru is the source of peace and love and is who you really are.

ALTERNATE BREATH EXERCISE

The opposing energy poles of the body: Uatchet (Udjat, Utchat) and Nekhebet (Ida and Pingala) can be balanced by practicing a simple alternate nostril breathing exercise. This is accomplished as follows: Using the right hand, bend the index and middle finger toward the palm while leaving the thumb, fourth and fifth (pinkie) fingers extended. Using the thumb to close off the right nostril, breath in (inhalation) through the left nostril while holding the right one closed, then close both nostrils using the fourth finger to close the left nostril leaving the pinkie finger extended and the other two fingers remaining bent. Release the thumb from the right nostril and exhale through the right nostril. Next breath in through the right nostril while holding the left one closed. Retain the breath for a short time, then breathe out through the left nostril. This constitutes one cycle of the Alternate nostril breathing exercise. The ratio of inhalation: retention: exhalation should be 2:8:4 to begin, working up to 4:16:8. You may repeat a mantra, hekau while performing this exercise. Continue in this way for five minutes at the beginning and then gradually building up to fifteen minutes or longer as needed. Then practice the physical exercises followed by the desired form of meditation of your choice. The Alternate breathing exercise is an excellent way to balance the body energies. The energies may also be balanced in a variety of other ways, such as controlling the emotions and remaining calm, engaging one's self in activities that are in harmony with one's consciousness (work, hobbies, job, recreation).

WORDS OF POWER IN MEDITATION

Hekau - Mantra Repetition:

Hekau-mantra recitation, (called *Japa* in India), is especially useful in changing the mental state. The sounds coupled with ideas or meditations can have the effect of calming the mind by directing its energy toward sublime thoughts rather than toward degrading, pain filled ones. This allows the vibrations of the mind to be changed. There are three types of recitation that can be used with the words of power: 1- Mental, 2- Recitation employing a soft humming sound and 3- loud or audible reciting. The main purpose of reciting the words of power is somewhat different than prayer. Prayer involves you as a subject, "talking" to God, while words of power - hekau - mantras, are used to carry your consciousness to divine levels by changing the vibrations in your mind and allowing it to transcend the awareness of the senses, body and ordinary thought processes.

The recitation of words of power has been explored to such a degree that it constitutes an important form of yoga practice. Two of the most comprehensive books written on this subject by Sri Swami Sivananda were *Japa Yoga* and *Sadhana.* Swami Sivananda told his pupils to repeat their mantras as many as 50,000 per day. If this level of practice is maintained, it is possible to achieve specific changes in a short time. Otherwise, changes in your level of mental awareness, self-control, mental peace and spiritual realization occur according to your level of practice. You should not rush nor suppress your spiritual development, rather allow it to gradually grow into a fire which engulfs the mind as your spiritual aspiration grows in a natural way.

Hekau - mantras can be directed toward worldly attainments or toward spiritual attainment in the form of enlightenment. There are words of power for gaining wealth or control over others. We will present Egyptian words of power which are directed to self-control and mental peace leading to spiritual realization of the Higher Self. You may choose from the list according to your level of understanding and practice. If you were initiated into a particular hekau or mantra by an authentic spiritual preceptor, we recommend that you use that one as your main meditative sound formula. You may use others for singing according to your inclination in your leisure or idle time. Also you may use shortened versions for chanting

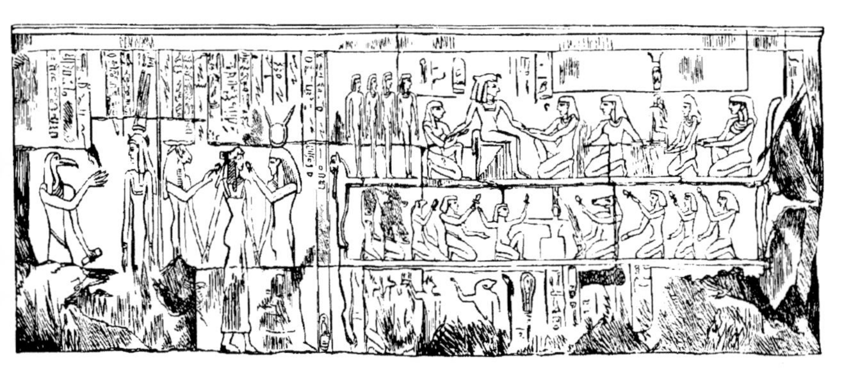

or singing when not engaged in formal practice. For example, if you choose "Om Amun Ra Ptah", you may also use "Om Amun" for short as well.

Words of power are like making a well. If a well is made deep enough, it yields water. If the words of power are used long enough and with consistency, they yield spiritual vibrations which reach deep into the unconscious mind to cut through the distracting thoughts and then reveal the deeper you. If they are not used with consistency, they are like a shallow puddles which get filled easily by rain, not having had a chance to go deeply enough to reveal what lies within. Mental recitation is considered to be the most powerful. However, in the beginning you may need to start with recitation aloud until you are able to control the mind's wandering. If it wanders, simply return to the words of power. Eventually the words of power will develop their own staying power. You will even hear them when you are not consciously reciting. They will begin to replace the negative thought patterns of the mind and lead the mind toward serenity and from here to spiritual realization.

When this begins to occur you should allow yourself to feel the sweetness of reciting the divine names. At times, after reciting for some time, you will experience that the words of power drop from your mind and there are no thoughts but just awareness. At that point your mind will disengage from all external exercises and take flight into the unknown, uncharted waters of the subconscious, the unconscious, and beyond. Simply remain as a detached witness and allow yourself to grow in peace. This is the soul level where you begin to transcend thoughts and body identification. You may use a rosary or mala (beads on a string) to keep track of your recitation.

As discussed earlier, HEKAU, or words of power may be used to achieve control over the mind and to develop the latent forces that are within you. Hekau or mantras are mystic formulas which an aspirant uses in a process of self-alchemy. The chosen words of power may be in the form of a letter, word or a combination of words which hold a specific mystical meaning which lead the mind to deeper levels of concentration and to deeper levels of understanding of the teaching behind the words. Listed below are several hekau taken from ancient Egyptian texts. They may be used in English or in ancient Kemetic according to your choice.

If you feel a certain affinity toward a particular energy expressed through a particular deity, use that inclination to your advantage by aligning yourself with that energy and then directing it toward the divine Self within your heart. Never forget that while you are working with a particular deity in the beginning stages, your objective is to delve into the deeper mystical implications of the symbolic form and characteristics of the deity. These always refer to the transcendental Self which is beyond all deities. According to your level of advancement you may construct your own Hekau according to your own feeling and understanding. As a rule, in meditations such as those being discussed now, the shorter the size of the hekau the more effective it will be since you will be able repeat it more often. However, the shorter the hekau, the more concentration it requires so as not to get lost in thoughts. Words of power have no power in and of themselves. It is the user who gives them power through understanding and feeling.

While *Om* is most commonly known as a *Sanskrit* mantra (word of power from India), it also appears in the ancient Egyptian texts and is closely related to the Kemetic *Amun* in sound and Amen of Christianity. More importantly, it has the same meaning as Amun and is therefore completely compatible with the energy pattern of the entire group. According to the Egyptian Leyden papyrus, the name of the "Hidden God", referring to Amun, may be pronounced as *Om,* or *Am*.

Om is a powerful sound because it is close to the primordial sound of creation. Om may also be used for engendering mental calm prior to beginning recitation of a longer set of words of power or it may be used alone as described above. One Indian tantric scripture (*Tattva*

Prakash) states that Om or AUM can be used to achieve the mental state free of physical identification and can bring union with *Brahman* (the Absolute transcendental Supreme Being - God) if it is repeated 300,000 times. In this sense, hekau- mantras such as Om, Amun, Nuk pu Neter, etc. are called Liberation or Salvation hekau or mantras which lead to union with the Absolute Self. Their shortness promotes greater concentration and force toward the primordial level of consciousness.

Simply choose a hekau which you feel comfortable with and sit quietly to recite it continuously for a set amount of time. Allow it to gradually become part of your free time when you are not concentrating on anything specific or when you are being distracted by worldly thoughts. This will serve to counteract the worldly or subconscious vibrations that may emerge from the your own unconscious. When you feel anger or other negative qualities present, recite the hekau and visualize its energy and the deity associated with it destroying the negativity.

For example, you may choose ***Amun-Ra-Ptah.*** When you repeat this hekau you are automatically including the entire system of all gods and goddesses. Amun-Ra-Ptah is known as ***Nebertcher*** the "All-encompassing Divinity". You may begin by uttering them aloud.

When you become more advanced in controlling your mind, you may begin to use shorter words. For example simply utter: *Amun, Amun, Amun...* always striving to get to the source of the sound. Eventually you will utter these silently and this practice will carry your consciousness to the source of the sound itself, to the place before its beginning, where the very mental instruction to utter is given. Hekau-mantras are related to the spiritual energy centers of the subtle spiritual body (Uraeus-Kundalini).

INTEGRATED MEDITATION

As stated in the beginning of this section there are four main components of meditation: posture, breath-life force control, sound and visualization. The previous meditation exercises have touched upon these areas but here we will use them all in an integrated fashion to achieve maximum concentration.

Before you begin, practice some light physical exercises (yoga, tai chi, etc.) for several minutes. This will serve to free up any energy blockages and wake up the mind by stimulating the circulation of the vital forces within the body.

Now choose a comfortable posture. If you have been practicing for some time, you will be able to gradually stay in one position for longer periods of time. If you practice regularly you will discover that your body will develop a daily rhythm which will be conducive to your meditation time. Next practice alternate nostril breathing so as to harmonize the positive and negative energies within the body. You may choose a hekau of your choice, one you feel especially drawn to and one that you understand the deeper meaning of to some degree or the one suggested by your spiritual preceptor. Repeat it with meaning and feeling as you breath and remain steady in your pose. This will serve the purpose of helping to occupy the attention of the mind and prevent it from straying and it will also help you to develop sensitivity and control over the vital energy so that eventually you will be able to direct it according to your will.

In the beginning it may seem as though not much is happening but within a short time you will begin to notice changes within yourself. Your level of relaxation will improve immediately and your awareness of yourself will increase gradually. Eventually, you will begin to perceive various new sensations and psychic expansion. You will hear your heart beat. A feeling of peacefulness will develop. You will not feel your arms or legs. This is an initial stage of transcendence. When you succeed in transcending your body consciousness you will be going beyond the exercises. Your inner vision will open and you will perceive reality beyond the mind and body. At this point do not worry about the components of the meditation. Simply relax and remain a witness to all you perceive. Do not try to run away from or to anything you notice. Gradually allow yourself to go deeper and deeper until you become one with the source of all thoughts. This is the real you. Continue practicing this "communion" exercise with the divine until you are fully established in this level of being at all times. This is the state of Enlightenment.

Recommended reading:

Meditation The Ancient Egyptian Path to Enlightenment– by Muata Ashby

The Glorious Lighte Meditation System of Ancient Egypt– by Muata Ashby

EGYPTIAN PROVERBS

The following ancient Egyptian selections come from the ***"Book of Coming Forth by Day"***:

Nuk pu NETER
I am the Supreme Divinity.

Nuk pu Ast
I am ISIS

nuk neter aa kheper tchesef
I am the great God, self created,

Ba ar pet sat ar ta.
Soul is of heaven, body belongs to the earth.

Nuk uab-k uab ka-k uab ba-k uab sekhem.
My mind has pure thoughts, so my soul and life forces are pure.

Nuk ast au neheh ertai-nef tetta.
Behold I am the heir of eternity, everlastingness has been given to me.

Sekhem - a em mu ma aua Set.
I have gained power in the water as I conquered Set (greed, lust, ignorance).

Rex - a em Ab - a sekhem - a em hati - a.
I know my heart, I have gained power over my heart.

Un - na uat neb am pet am ta.
The power is within me to open all doors in heaven and earth.

Nuk sah em ba - f.
I am a spirit, with my soul.

The following ancient Egyptian selections come from the ***"Pyramid Texts of Unas"*** (you may substitute your name where *Unas* appears):

Unas pa neb sabut
Unas is the lord (mistress) of wisdom

au aart - f em apt -f
His Uraei are on his brow

Unas pa aper-a er aab khu - f
Unas is provided with power over his spirits

au Unas kha em ur pu
Unas rises (to heaven) like a mighty one

Unas pu neb hetep
Unas is the lord of the offering

Unas pa am heka - sen
Unas has eaten the words of power of the gods

Unas aam khu - sen
Unas has eaten the spirits of the gods

Recitation of the name of the divine can be performed as a means to control the mind and direct it toward the divine.

Nebertcher
All encompassing existence
(The Absolute)

Amun-Ra-Ptah
The holy Trinity

GLOSSARY

AIEMHETEP; IMHOTEP; ASCLEPIUS(Greek): Celebrated physician of Memphis. Builder of the first pyramid. Deified as a god of medicine and surgery.

AMENTA: Underworld; where souls who have passed on from the earthly plane traverse and are judged as to their virtue.

AMI-UT: Dweller of the embalment chamber, a title of ANUBIS.(see ANUBIS).

APIABU: "counter of hearts", a name of ANUBIS.(see ANUBIS)

BENU: The Phoenix who, upon incineration, rises renewed from the ashes.

FATHER-MOTHER CREATOR GOD: The originator, maker of all things, the one called by many names in many religions as the only one; the essence of everything; the Great Spirit,

DAIMONS: Administrators of the Gods who carry out duties in the lower spheres of existence. "the duty of the daimons is to give requital." through "good" or "bad" activity since a Daimon's job is activity on behalf of the Gods.

FACE: Unmanifest True divine essence of the being achieved through spiritual growth.

GNOSIS: Experiential knowledge of the transcendent/divine. see Knowing below.

GODS: Advanced souls with great capabilities to carry out the work of the Creator. Children created by the Creator. What wise humans aspire to be.

HEKAU: Words of Power

HORUS: The brother/nephew of SETHAN, restorer of truth and justice(MAAT).

IN THE HORIZON: Subtle realm over which Osiris has influence and power to grant life to the dead from our physical realm.

ISIS, AUSET, AST: Goddess of motherhood, nurturing. Mother of HORUS, dweller in Sothis., resurrector of Osiris.

KHEPERA: The God represented by the nile scarab, ever transforming from season to season, coming into the light, as we, engaged in the cycle of rebirth, ever transform from death to life again.

KMT: (Pronounced Kamit or Kemet) Ancient name of Egypt as named by its indigenous inhabitants, the Afrikans later called Hamitic (Black skinned) peoples by Asians(People from the area now called Arabia, Iraq, Iran, etc.) and Eurasians(Greeks, Romans, French, English, etc.). The Black Land, Land of Blackness; Primordial Blackness, Opaqueness, from which all comes(creation); Land of the Black people. Foremost is Osiris, redeemer, bestower of everlasting life, He is known as "THE GREAT BLACK"

KNOWING: Having information and Having knowledge are not necessarily the same thing. Much in the WORLD is information we are told, much is information gathered by our senses which are made to gather information from the physical realm only.

Since human senses are designed to perceive physical objects, they miss a whole other reality which lies beyond. The "Absolute Truth" or God which underlies all things in the "physical" realm cannot be sensed with the ordinary senses which are designed only for the world of duality.

The universe of male - female, ying - yang, up - down, came from the real of homogeneity, grayness, timelessness, bottomlessness, boundlessness, etc. All limitations of the physical realm came from the limitless realm of the Spirit. This is made perfectly clear in the earliest Cosmogenical scriptures.

Therefore, human senses, which are created and exist in the physical universe will be useless in perceiving the Spirit. The change must be within the mind and heart of the individual. The individual must change into the Spirit in order to see the Spirit.

LOGOS: Sermon; discourse; reason; The word; uttered by god which created and maintains creation; universal truth.

LONG LIVED: Herein refers to longevity in the spiritual realm, not the physical-temporal.

MAAT: Truth, Justice, correctness, righteousness; which cannot be separated from both it's doing and it's speaking. If one does not do *MAAT*, one cannot speak it and vise versa.

MER: Pyramid, House of Fire

MIN: The god of fertility, and strength of will depicted with erect phallus showing vitality and a raised flail to control it in wisdom .

NAMES: The Egyptian language is that of power; not words, sounds fulfilled with deeds, the very Power of the Egyptian Names, have in themselves the Power to bring into act what is said.

NETER: God principle, divine manifestation, divine entity assisting the Creator in the management of creation.

NETERS: (Divine causal principals-Gods and God's aspects-forces which operate within creation)

NETERU: Gods: divine powers latent within humans, divine ways.

OSIRIS (ASAR, AUSAR, ASR): The god of eternal life and reincarnation. The goal state of the seeker of self and godhood through knowledge and wisdom. The title "AUSAR" is given to the successful initiates into the light of self knowledge.

PARTS OF THE SOUL-SPIRIT
(1) The KA: The abstract personality, ethereal body possessing power of locomotion.
(2) THE KHAT: The concrete personality, the physical body.
(3) THE BA: The heart-soul which dwells in the KA with power of metamorphosis.
(4) THE AB: Heart, the animal life in man, rational, spiritual, ethical, undergoes examination by Osiris in the Book of Coming forth by day.
(5) THE KHAIBIT: Shadow, associated with the BA from whom it receives nourishment and has power of locomotion and omnipresence.
(6) THE KHU: Spiritual Soul, which is immortal; associated with the BA and is an Ethereal Being.
(7) THE SAHU: Spiritual body in which the KHU dwells; The spiritual and mental attributes of the natural body are united to the new powers of it's own nature.
(8) THE SEKHEM: Power; spiritual personification of the vital force in man and woman; It's dwelling place is in the heavens with the KHUS.
(9) THE REN: The name; essential attribute to the personification of a being; The name sometimes found encircled by a rope of light called a cartouche which is also associated with the Shen which is associated with the top part of the Ankh Symbol. A rope of Sunlight or life force harnessed into the form of a circle, the most impregnable structure to protect the name against attack.

Sanctuary of God; The Temple not made with hands; Temple of the human spirit: The human body.

SEKHEM OR SHEKEM: Power, complete control will to manifest what is desired.

SETHAN: The God who was originally good and later turned to evil, becoming the precursor of "SATAN", "CAIN" and the modern "DEVIL".

Sucha Daudi: Come forth Djehuti; come forth wisdom; into my Soul Spirit, that I may do the will of God, the Supreme Being on Earth.

EGYPTIAN PROVERBS

TA-MERRY: Ancient name of Egypt as named by its indigenous inhabitants, the Afrikans later called Hamitic(Black skinned) peoples by Asians(People from the area now called Arabia, Iraq, Iran, etc.) and Eurasians(Greeks, Romans, French, English, etc.).

TEMT TCHAAS: a collection or book of sayings containing the primeval wisdom of ancient times.

THE GOOD: God, Supreme Being, The All.

TITAN: Rulers of the earthly world order; government, social, religious etc. leaders.

TYPHON: is the passionate, titanic, reasonless and impulsive aspect of the soul, while of the corporeal side, the death dealing, pestilent and disturbing, with reasonable times.

VIRTUE: Any actions that are beneficial to ones self, the family, society, the world and to the universe.

INDEX

Bibliography

All sayings used in this volume were taken from the following sources.

1– Pert Em Heru (Book of Coming Forth by Day – Ancient Egyptian Book of the Dead)

The Papyrus of Ani
The Papyrus of Anhai
The Papyrus of Hunefer
The Papyrus of Qenna
The Papyrus of Nu
And other Hieroglyphic texts.

2– The Ancient Egyptian Pyramid Texts

The Pyramid of Unas
The Pyramid of Pepi

3– The Ancient Egyptian Wisdom Texts

The Precepts of Ptahotep
The Instructions of Ani
The Instructions of Amenemope
The Instructions of Merikara
The Teachings of Kaqemna
And other Hieroglyphic texts.

4– Wisdom Teachings Ascribed to Akhenaton (Sage King of Ancient Egypt)

Hyms to Aton

5– Thrice Greatest Hermes – The Wisdom Teachings ascribed to the Ancient Egyptian God Djehuti.

6– The Kybalion — The Wisdom Teachings ascribed to the Ancient Egyptian God Djehuti..

All Hieroglyphic text and graphics available through the Scribesoft Collection for the PC, designed by Muata Ashby Cruzian Mystic Books LTD.

Cruzian Mystic P.O.Box 570459, Miami, Florida. 33257 (305) 378-6253, Fax. (305) 378-6253

New Release

THE EGYPTIAN BOOK OF THE DEAD
Mysticism of the
Pert Em Heru
By
Dr. Muata Ashby
$24.95 ISBN# 1-884564-28-3
Size: 8½" X 11" - 326 Pages

I Know myself, I know myself, I am One With God!
–From the Pert Em Heru

"The Ru Pert em Heru" or "Ancient Egyptian Book of The Dead," or "Book of Coming Forth By Day" as it is more popularly known, has fascinated the world since the successful translation of Ancient Egyptian hieroglyphic scripture over 150 years ago. The astonishing writings in it reveal that the Ancient Egyptians believed in life after death and in an ultimate destiny to discover the Divine. The elegance and aesthetic beauty of the hieroglyphic text itself has inspired many see it as an art form in and of itself.
But is there more to it than that? Did the Ancient Egyptian wisdom contain more than just aphorisms and hopes of eternal life beyond death?
In this volume Dr. Muata Ashby, the author of over 25 books on Ancient Egyptian Yoga Philosophy has produced a new translation of the original texts which uncovers a mystical teaching underlying the sayings and rituals instituted by the Ancient Egyptian Sages and Saints.
"Once the philosophy of Ancient Egypt is understood as a mystical tradition instead of as a religion or primitive mythology, it reveals its secrets which if practiced today will lead anyone to discover the glory of spiritual self-discovery. The Pert em Heru is in every way comparable to the Indian Upanishads or the Tibetan Book of the Dead."
– Muata Abhaya Ashby

OTHER BOOKS BY MUATA ASHBY
THE YOGA AND MYSTICAL SPIRITUALITY BOOK SERIES
Available through C .M. Books

(A)
EGYPTIAN YOGA:
THE PHILOSOPHY OF ENLIGHTENMENT

An original, fully illustrated work, including hieroglyphs, detailing the meaning of the Egyptian mysteries, tantric yoga, psycho-spiritual and physical exercises. Egyptian Yoga is a guide to the practice of the highest spiritual philosophy which leads to absolute freedom from human misery and to immortality. It is well known by scholars that Egyptian philosophy is the basis of Western and Middle Eastern religious philosophies such as *Christianity, Islam, Judaism,* the *Kabbalah*, and Greek philosophy, but what about Indian philosophy, Yoga and Taoism? What were the original teachings? How can they be practiced today? What is the source of pain and suffering in the world and what is the solution? Discover the deepest mysteries of the mind and universe within and outside of your self.
216 Pages 8.5" X 11" ISBN: 1-884564-01-1 Soft $18.95 U.S.

(A-1)
EGYPTIAN YOGA II
The Supreme Wisdom of Enlightenment

In this long awaited sequel to ***Egyptian Yoga: The Philosophy of Enlightenment*** you will take a fascinating and enlightening journey back in time and discover the teachings which constituted the epitome of Ancient Egyptian spiritual wisdom. What is the supreme knowledge knowing which nothing is left unknown? What are the disciplines which lead to the fulfillment of all desires? Delve into the three states of consciousness (waking, dream and deep sleep) and the fourth state which transcends them all, Neberdjer, "The Absolute." These teachings of the city of Waset (Thebes) were the crowning achievement of the Sages of Ancient Egypt. They summarize and comprehensively explain the mysteries of the entire symbolism of the Ancient Egyptian pantheon of gods and goddesses that emanate from a Supreme Being who forms Creation while emerging as a Trinity. They establish the standard mystical keys for understanding the profound mystical symbolism of the Triad of human consciousness manifesting as the Trinity of gods, Amun-Ra-Ptah, symbolizing the mysticism of the soul, the mind, and creation, respectively. **ISBN 1-884564-39-9 8.5" X 11" $18.95 U.S.**

(B)

THE AUSARIAN RESURRECTION:
The Ancient Egyptian Bible

The Ancient Sages created stories based on human and superhuman beings whose struggles, aspirations, needs and desires ultimately lead them to discover their true Self. The myth of Isis, Osiris and Horus is no exception in this area. While there is no one source where the entire story may be found, pieces of it are inscribed in various ancient temples walls, tombs, steles and papyri. For the first time available, the complete myth of Osiris, Isis and Horus has been compiled from original Ancient Egyptian, Greek and Coptic Texts. This epic myth has been richly illustrated with reliefs from the temple of Horus at Edfu, the temple of Isis at Philae, the temple of Osiris at Abydos, the temple of Hathor at Denderah and various papyri, inscriptions and reliefs.

Discover the myth which inspired the teachings of the *Shetaut Neter* (Egyptian Mystery System - Egyptian Yoga) and the Egyptian Book of Coming Forth By Day. Also, discover the three levels of Ancient Egyptian Religion, how to understand the mysteries of the Tuat or Astral World and how to discover the abode of the Supreme in the Amenta, *The Other World.*

The ancient religion of Osiris, Isis and Horus, if properly understood, contains all of the elements necessary to lead the sincere aspirant to attain immortality through inner self-discovery. This volume presents the entire myth and explores the main mystical themes and rituals associated with the myth for understating human existence, creation and the way to achieve spiritual emancipation - *Resurrection.* The Osirian myth is so powerful that it influenced and is still having an effect on the major world religions. Discover the origins and mystical meaning of the Christian Trinity, the Eucharist ritual and the ancient origin of the birthday of Jesus Christ.
200 Pages 8.5" X 11" Hard Cover ISBN: 1-884564-12-7 $29.99 U.S. Soft Cover ISBN: 1-884564-27-5 $18.95

(C)
THE MYSTICAL TEACHINGS
OF
THE AUSARIAN RESURRECTION

This Volume will detail the myth of the Osirian Resurrection and The Story of Horus and Set and their mystical implications in the life of the aspirant/initiate. Then this volume will turn to a line by line mystical reading of the myth in order to uncover the mystical implications of the epic story. Mythology will come alive as a message from the Sages of ancient times to the initiates and not just as stories for entertainment. This Volume is special because it links the individual student to the myth and thereby gives her/him deep insight into his/her own true nature and how to practice the religion of Osiris, Isis and Horus. This volume may be used as a companion to the book

The Ausarian Resurrection: The Ancient Egyptian Bible by Muata Ashby (see the description above). **232 pages 5.5"x 8.5" ISBN: 1-884564-22-4 $15.99**

(D)
THE PROPERTIES OF MATTER:
Egyptian Physics and
Yoga Metaphysics.

This Volume will go deeper into the philosophy of God as creation and will explore the concepts of modern science and how they correlate with ancient teachings. This Volume will lay the ground work for the understanding of the philosophy of universal consciousness and the initiatic/yogic insight into who or what is God? **200 pages. 5.5"x 8.5" ISBN 1-884564-07-0 $14.99**

(E)
INITIATION INTO EGYPTIAN YOGA:
The Secrets of Sheti

Sheti: Spiritual discipline or program, to go deeply into the mysteries, to study the mystery teachings and literature profoundly, to penetrate the mysteries.

☥ You will learn about the mysteries of initiation into the teachings and practice of Yoga and how to become an Initiate of the mystical sciences.

This insightful manual is the first in a series which introduces you to the goals of daily spiritual and yoga practices: Meditation, Diet, Words of Power and the ancient wisdom teachings.
150 pages 8.5" X 11" ISBN 1-884564-02-X Soft Cover $16.99 U.S.

(F)
THE GLORY OF INITIATION

A brief discussion of the theme of Initiation which was introduced in the book *Initiation Into Egyptian Yoga.* This volume explores the need for initiation and how a person is initiated into the teachings of mystical spirituality. Many new important topics are introduced such as: The Ancient Egyptian "Guru," The Mystical Sphinx, The Life of an Initiate of Yoga, The Importance of the Spiritual Name, Initiation With a Spiritual Preceptor and The Initiation Ritual. 40 pages $3.99 ISBN: 1-884564-37- 2

(G)
THE WISDOM OF ISIS
GOD IN THE UNIVERSE, GOD IN THE HEART
Who is God in the light of
Yoga Philosophy?

EGYPTIAN PROVERBS

Through the study of ancient myth and the illumination of initiatic understanding the idea of God is expanded from the mythological comprehension to the metaphysical. Then this metaphysical understanding is related to you, the student, so as to begin understanding your true divine nature. **243 pages 5.5"x 8.5" ISBN 1-884564-24-0 $15.99**

(H)
THE PATH OF DIVINE LOVE
The Process of Mystical Transformation and The Path of Divine Love

This Volume will focus on the ancient wisdom teachings and how to use them in a scientific process for self-transformation. Also, this volume will detail the process of transformation from ordinary consciousness to cosmic consciousness through the integrated practice of the teachings and the path of Devotional Love toward the Divine. **225 pages 5.5"x 8.5" ISBN 1-884564-11-9 $15.99**

(I)
THE WISDOM OF MAATI:
Spiritual Enlightenment Through the Path of Virtue

Known as Karma Yoga in India, the teachings of MAAT for living virtuously and with orderly wisdom are explained and the student is to begin practicing the precepts of Maat in daily life so as to promote the process of purification of the heart in preparation for the judgment of the soul. This judgment will be understood not as an event that will occur at the time of death but as an event that occurs continuously, at every moment in the life of the individual. The student will learn how to become allied with the forces of the Higher Self and to thereby begin cleansing the mind (heart) of impurities so as to attain a higher vision of reality. 210 **pages 5.5"x 8.5" ISBN 1-884564-20-8 $15.99**

(J)
MEDITATION
The Ancient Egyptian Path to Enlightenment

Many people do not know about the rich history of meditation practice in Ancient Egypt. This volume outlines the theory of meditation and presents the Ancient Egyptian Hieroglyphic text which give instruction as to the nature of the mind and its three modes of expression. It also presents the texts which give instruction on the practice of meditation for spiritual enlightenment and unity with the Divine. This volume allows the reader to begin practicing meditation by explaining, in easy to understand terms, the simplest form of meditation and working up to the most advanced form which was practiced in ancient times and which is still practiced by yogis around the world in modern times. **268 pages 5.5"x 8.5" ISBN 1-884564-27-7 $16.99**

(K)
EGYPTIAN TANTRA YOGA:
The Art of Sex Sublimation and Universal Consciousness

This Volume will expand on the male and female principles within the human body and in the universe and further detail the sublimation of sexual energy into spiritual energy. The student will study the deities Min and Hathor, Osiris and Isis, Geb and Nut and discover the mystical implications for a practical spiritual discipline. This Volume will also focus on the Tantric aspects of Ancient Egyptian and Indian mysticism, the purpose of sex and the mystical teachings of sexual sublimation which lead to self-knowledge and enlightenment. **243 pages 5.5"x 8.5"**
ISBN 1-884564-03-8 $15.99

(L)
MYSTICISM OF USHET REKHAT:
Worship of the Divine Mother

The Supreme Being may be worshipped as father or as mother. *Ushet Rekhat* or *Mother Worship*, is the spiritual process of worshipping the Divine in the form of the Divine Goddess. It celebrates the most important forms of the Goddess including *Nathor, Maat, Aset, Arat, Amentet and Hathor* and explores their mystical meaning as well as the rising of *Sirius,* the star of Aset (Isis) and the new birth of Hor (Horus). The end of the year is a time of reckoning, reflection and engendering a new or renewed positive movement toward attaining spiritual enlightenment. The Mother Worship devotional meditation ritual, performed on five days during the month of December and on New Year's Eve, is based on the Ushet Rekhit. During the ceremony, the cosmic forces, symbolized by Sirius ★ and the constellation of Orion ★★★, are harnessed through the understanding and devotional attitude of the participant. This propitiation draws the light of wisdom and health to all those who share in the ritual, leading to prosperity and wisdom.
$9.99 - 146 pages. 5.5"x 8.5" ISBN 1-884564-18-6

(M)
HEALING THE CRIMINAL HEART
Introduction to Maat Philosophy, Yoga and Spiritual Redemption Through the Path of Virtue

Who is a criminal? Is there such a thing as a criminal heart? What is the source of evil and sinfulness and is there any way to rise above it? Is there redemption for those who have committed sins, even the worst crimes?

Ancient Egyptian mystical psychology holds important answers to these questions. Over ten thousand years ago mystical psychologists, the Sages of Ancient Egypt, studied and charted the human mind and spirit and laid out a path which will lead to spiritual redemption, prosperity and enlightenment.
This introductory volume brings forth the teachings of the Ausarian Resurrection, the most important myth of Ancient Egypt, with relation to the faults of human existence: anger, hatred, greed, lust, animosity, discontent, ignorance, egoism jealousy, bitterness, and a myriad of psycho-spiritual ailments which keep a human being in a state of negativity and adversity.
40 pages 5.5"x 8.5" ISBN: 1-884564-17-8 $3.99

(N)
EGYPTIAN YOGA EXERCISE WORKOUT BOOK
Thef Neteru:
The Movement of The Gods and Goddesses

Discover the physical postures and exercises practiced thousands of years ago in Ancient Egypt which are today known as Yoga exercises. This work is based on the pictures and teachings from the Creation story of Ra, The Osirian Resurrection Myth and the carvings and reliefs from various Temples in Ancient Egypt. **145 Pages 8.5" X 11" ISBN 1-884564-10-0 Soft Cover $16.99** **Exercise video $19.99**

(O)
THE SERPENT POWER:
The Ancient Egyptian Mystical Wisdom of the Inner Life Force.

This Volume specifically deals with the latent life Force energy of the universe and in the human body, its control and sublimation. How to develop the Life Force energy of the subtle body. This Volume will introduce the esoteric wisdom of the science of how virtuous living acts in a subtle and mysterious way to cleanse the latent psychic energy conduits and vortices of the spiritual body. **204 pages 5.5"x 8.5" ISBN 1-884564-19-4 $15.99**

(P)
THE CYCLES OF TIME:

EGYPTIAN PROVERBS

The Ancient Origins of Yoga in Egypt and India

This Volume will cover the ancient origins of Yoga and establish a link between the cultures of Ancient Egypt and ancient and modern India. This Volume is of paramount importance because it shows that Egyptian Philosophy began over 30,000 years ago and did not die out along with Egyptian society but that it was carried on by the Sages and Saints who left Egypt at the time of its social collapse. **200 pages. 5.5"x 8.5" ISBN 1-884564-13-5 $14.99**

(Q)
THE MYSTERIES OF SHETAUT PAUTI
The Mystical Teachings of The Ancient Egyptian Creation Myth

Discover the mystical teachings contained in the Creation Myth and the gods and goddesses who brought creation and human beings into existence. The Creation Myth holds the key to understanding the universe and for attaining spiritual enlightenment.
ISBN: 1-884564-38-0 40 pages $5.99

(R)
GROWING BEYOND HATE
The Mystic Art
of Transcending Hate and Discovering
Spiritual Enlightenment Through Yoga

What is the source of animosity between human beings? What is the basis for negativity in the human heart and is there a way to deal with it? How can the teachings of Yoga Philosophy be used to resolve animosity and to transcend hatred in order to attain spiritual enlightenment and promote harmony in society.

Human Relations is an important issue in modern times. This volume is an introductory guide to understanding why people engage in various forms of animosity including hatred, hostility, racism, sexism, etc. towards others. It provides insights into the nature of the mind and the process of spiritual development which leads to purity of heart and spiritual emancipation. 64 Pages ISBN: 1-884564-34-8 $5.99

(S)
THE SLOWNESS MEDITATION
How to Discover
The Inner Witnessing Self

The Slowness meditation is the art of concentrating on movement and discovering the inner light of the Self

What is the *Inner Witnessing Self* and how can slowness lead a person to discover it? What is *automatic consciousness* and what does it operate in the mind of most human beings?
Discover the discipline of meditation which will allow you to go beyond the mundane realities of life so that you may discover inner peace, expansion of consciousness, inner fulfillment and contentment.
This is the Slowness Meditation Program 40 Pages ISBN: 1-884564-36-4
$4.99

(T)
THE STORY OF ASAR, ASET AND HERU:
An Ancient Egyptian Legend

Now for the first time, the most ancient myth of Ancient Egypt comes alive for children. Inspired by the books *The Ausarian Resurrection: The Ancient Egyptian Bible* and *The Mystical Teachings of The Ausarian Resurrection,* ***The Story of Asar, Aset and Heru*** is an easy to understand and thrilling tale which inspired the children of Ancient Egypt to aspire to greatness and righteousness.

If you and your child have enjoyed stories like *The Lion King* and *Star Wars you will love* ***The Story of Asar, Aset and Heru.*** Also, if you know the story of Jesus and Krishna you will discover than Ancient Egypt had a similar myth and that this myth carries important spiritual teachings for living a fruitful and fulfilling life.

This book may be used along with ***The Parents Guide To The Ausarian Resurrection Myth: How to Teach Yourself and Your Child the Principles of Universal Mystical Religion.*** The guide provides some background to the Ausarian Resurrection myth and it also gives insight into the mystical teachings contained in it which you may introduce to your child. It is designed for parents who wish to grow spiritually with their children and it serves as an introduction for those who would like to study the Ausarian Resurrection Myth in depth and to practice its teachings. **41 pages 8.5" X 11" ISBN: 1-884564-31-3 $8.99**

(U)
THE PARENTS GUIDE TO THE AUSARIAN RESURRECTION MYTH:
How to Teach Yourself and Your Child
the Principles of Universal Mystical Religion.

This insightful manual brings for the timeless wisdom of the ancient through the Ancient Egyptian myth of Asar, Aset and Heru and the mystical teachings contained in it for parents who want to guide their children to

understand and practice the teachings of mystical spirituality. This manual may be used with the children's storybook *The Story of Asar, Aset and Heru* by Dr. Muata Abhaya Ashby. **64 pages 5.5"x 8.5"**
ISBN: 1-884564-30-5 $5.99

For a complete listing of titles send for the free ***Egyptian Yoga Catalog***

AUDIO LECTURE SERIES BY DR. MUATA ASHBY

All **cassettes on Sale for only $ 9.99**

Use the number when ordering.

Wisdom of Egyptian Yoga
100 Introduction to Egyptian Yoga, the paths of Yoga and Mystical Religion 9/15/97 $9.99
100A-100B Introduction to Egyptian Yoga, the paths of Yoga and Mystical Religion 2 tapes $14.99
102 What is Yoga and how can it transform your life? Radio Interview in LA - $4.99
103 Wisdom of Egyptian Yoga Part 1 $9.99 - 90min (103 & 104 - 2 tape set)
104 Wisdom of Egyptian Yoga Part 2 $9.99 - 90min (103 & 104 - 2 tape set)
105 Maat Workshop Part 1: How to Practice the Teachings - $9.99- 90min
106 Maat Workshop Part 2: How to Practice the Teachings -$9.99- 90min
107 Pert Em Heru: Introduction to the Book of Coming Forth By Day Part 1-$9.99
108 Pert Em Heru: Introduction to the Book of Coming Forth By Day Part 2-$9.99
109 Initiation Into Shetaut Aset Part 1: The Teachings of The Temple of Isis- $9.99
110 Initiation Into Shetaut Aset Part 2: The Teachings of The Temple of Isis - $9.99
111 The Cycles of Time - $14.99 - 2 hours
112 Race Relations in the light of Yoga Philosophy $9.99 - 90 min
113 Nature Of Embodiment
114 Seven Steps Of Maat
115 Cycles of Time – Study of History from the Mystical perspective.
116A Indus Kamit Kush Part 1
116B Indus Kamit Kush Part 2

The process of Initiation and the Initiatic Way of Life
200 Initiation Into Egyptian Yoga Part I- $9.99 (200 & 201 - 2 tape set) 90min
201 Initiation Into Egyptian Yoga Part II- $9.99 (200 & 201 - 2 tape set) 90 min.
209 Sheti Workshop Part 1
210 Sheti Workshop Part 2
211 The Initiatic Way Of Ed (Ohio) 2/9/97- $14.99 -Two hours

Initiation Series Class Lectures Based on the Book
203 CLASS 1 Initiation: How to be a Disciple of Yoga: - $9.99 - 90 min
204 CLASS 2 Initiation: The Ten Virtues of a Spiritual Aspirant Part 1 -$9.99- 60 min (204 & 205 set)
205 CLASS 3 Initiation: The Ten Virtues of a Spiritual Aspirant Part 2 -$9.99 - 60 min (204 & 205 set)
206 CLASS 4 Introduction to Meditation: The Art of Concentration $9.99 - 60 min
207 CLASS 5 Initiation: Health, Vegetarianism and Yoga $9.99 - 90 min
212 Good Association – The Importance of and how to conduct the Sheti Group Study Meetings

Ausarian Resurrection Series 1997 Based on The Book Ausarian Resurrection: The Ancient Egyptian Bible
300 Ausarian Resurrection, (Presentation) Part 1- $9.99
301 Ausarian Resurrection, (Presentation) Part 2- $9.99
302 CLASS 1 The Three Levels of Religion - $9.99 - 90 min.
303 CLASS 2 The Story of Hethor and Djehuti: The Three States of Consciousness - $9.99 - 90 min.
304 CLASS 3 The Story of Ra and Aset $9.99 - 90 min.
305 CLASS 4 Understanding the mind and how to transcend the Ego $9.99
306 CLASS 5 The Glory of Devotional Love, Part 1 - $9.99 - 90 min
307 CLASS 6 The Glory of Devotional Love, Part 2 - $9.99 - 90 min
308 CLASS 7 The Birth of Heru & the Meaning of Happiness - $9.99 - 90 min
309 CLASS 8 The Death of Heru: How Egoism Poisons Spiritual Aspiration $9.99 - 90 min
310 CLASS 9 The Glory of Listening to the Teachings - $9.99 - 90 min
311 CLASS 10 The Initiation of Heru $9.99 - 90 min
312 CLASS 11 How the soul becomes incarnated and trapped in the body $9.99 - 60 min
313 CLASS 12 How the soul operated through mind and senses and ego $9.99 - 90 min
314 CLASS 13 How externalized senses lead to suffering and how suffering leads to enlightenment $9.99
315 CLASS 14 How Karma Works to Guide the Soul and How to overcome the warlike mentality $9.99
316 Class 15 Lecture 1/25/98 Verse 71 The Initiation of Heru
316B Class 15B Verse 86 The Nature of Human Embodiment
317 Class 16 3/8/98, Verse 95-110
318 Class 17 3/15/98, Verse 111-119
319 Class 18 3/22/98, Verse 120
320 Class 19 3/29/98, Illusory Nature Of World
321 Class 20 4/4/98, Verse 130
322 Class 21 Illusion of Desires, Tantrism, Sexuality and Enlightenment 4/26/98.
323 Class 22 5/3/98, Verse 145 The challenge of the Lower Self against three Higher Self
324-325 Class 23 Conclusion Two tape Set 5/10/98: Desperation, Sexuality, Spiritual Victory -Verse 163 to conclusion.

Daily Worship, Chanting, Devotional Practice.
501 Ushet Morning Worship: Adorations to Ra-Khepera and Hethor $9.99 - approx. 30 min.
502 Ushet Morning Worship: Adorations to Amun - $9.99 - 60 min.
503 Morning Worship Led By Vijaya
504 Morning Worship To Khepra and Midday worship to Ra
900 Ushet Devotional Chanting of Hekau *Amma Su En Pa Neter* - $9.99 - 60 min.
901 Ushet Devotional Chanting of Divine Name Hekau: *Om Amun Ra Ptah* - $9.99 - 60 min.
902 Ushet Devotional Chanting of Divine Name Hekau: *Om Asar, Aset, Heru* - $9.99 - 60 min.

Physical Exercise Workout
600 The Egyptian Yoga Exercise Workout with Vijaya Level I- short session $9.99 45 min.
601 The Egyptian Yoga Exercise Workout with Vijaya Level II- long session $9.99 - 90 min
603 The Egyptian Yoga Exercise Workout and Meditation with Muata Level III - long session $9.99 - 90 min
604 The Egyptian Yoga Exercise Workout with Muata Short session $9.99 30 min

Meditation Practice Based on the Book
700 Meditation Lecture Series Part 1 (St. Louis)- $9.99 -60 min. (700, 701 & 702 - 3 tape set)
701 Meditation Lecture Series, Part 2 (St. Louis) - $9.99 - 60 min. (700, 701 & 702 - 3 tape set)
702 Meditation Lecture Series, Part 3 (St. Louis) - $9.99 - 60 min. (700, 701 & 702 - 3 tape set)
703 Guided Meditation Session $9.99
704 Lotus Meditation (Vijaya), 6/27/98
705 Concentration-meditation session 15 minutes for use with the Initiation Class Lecture series.
706 Slowness Meditation Session
707 Meditation for Transcending Fear
800 Serpent Power Level I: Lecture, Music and Meditation -$9.99 - 90min
801 Serpent Power Level II: Lecture, Music and Meditation - $9.99 - 90min

Christian Yoga Based on the Book Christian Yoga
1000 Issues in Christian Yoga-Lecture at Unity Church in Los Angeles $9.99
1001-A Introduction to Christian Yoga: How to understand and Study the Book $9.99 (Part I)
1001-B Introduction to Christian Yoga: Questions and Answers about Christian Yoga (Part II)
1002 Orthodox Religion vs. Yoga Philosophy – resolving the conflict.

Advanced Teaching Series
2000 How To Teach yoga

Special Interest Lectures
3000 Mystic Poetry Readings by Dr. Ashby and students 3/15/98
3001 Creation of the Sema Institute of Yoga Temple 4/19/98
3002 Inspiration for Teenagers (dealing with anger, sex and discovering the purpose of life.)
3003 Inspiration for College students Set up Fraternities and Sororities based on original Egyptian Wisdom.
3004 Glory of Silence
3005-3008 Yoga and Mental Health Seminar (4 tapes)
3009-3010 Ancient Egyptian origins of Fraternities and Sorrorities and Western Culture and Philosophy (2 tapes)
3011 Spiritual Self-Publishing
3012 Dramatic Arts, Music and Enlightenment in Ancient Egyptian Theater

Maat Philosophy Series 1998 Lectures Maat, the 42 Laws, the Ancient Egyptian Wisdom Texts
4001 Class 1 - Introduction to Maat Philosophy
4002 Class 2 - Profound issues of Maat and its practice in life
4003 Class 3 - Profound issues and the Cycle of Vice
4004 Class 4 - Introduction to the Principle of Truth
4005 Class 5 - Principle of Truth Part 2
4006 Class 6 - Principle of Truth Part 3
4007 Class 7 - Principle of Truth part 4
4008 Class 8 - Introduction to the Principle of Non-violence
4009 Class 9 - Principle of Non-violence Part 2

4010 Class 10 - Principle of Non-violence Part 3
4011 Class 11 - Principle of Non-violence Part 4
4012 Class 12 – Principle of Non-stealing Part 1
4013 Class 13 – Principle of Non-stealing Part 2
4014 Class 14 – Principle of Non-stealing Part 3
4015 Class 15 – Principle of Selfless Service
4016 Class 16 – Principle of Right Action
4017 Class 17 – Principle of Right Speech Part 1
4018 Class 18 – Principle of Right Speech Part 2
4019 Class 19 – Principle of Right Speech Part 3
4020 Class 20 – Principle of Right Speech Part 4
4021 Class 21 – Principle of Right Worship Part 1
4022 Class 22 – Principle of Right Worship Part 2
4023 Class 23 – Principle of Right Worship Part 3
4024 Class 24 – Principle of Right Worship Part 4
4025 Class 25 – Principle of Right Worship Part 5
4026 Class 26 – Principle of Right Worship Part 6
4027 Class 25 – Principle of Right Thinking Part 1

Order Form

Telephone orders: Call Toll Free: 1(305) 378-6253. Have your AMEX, Optima, Visa or MasterCard ready.
Fax orders: 1-(305) 378-6253

Postal Orders: Sema Institute of Yoga, P.O. Box 570459, Miami, Fl. 33257. USA.

Please send the following books and / or tapes.

ITEM

______________________________ Cost $________
______________________________ Cost $________
______________________________ Cost $________
Total $________

_____Please send the latest *Egyptian Yoga Catalog* to me FREE.
_____Please add my name to the *Sheti Association* so that I may receive more
information on upcoming Yoga Seminars and other events.

Name:______________________________
Address:______________________________
City:__________________ State:_______ Zip:_________

Sales tax: Please add 6.5% for books shipped to Florida addresses

Shipping-.
________Book Rate: $2.00 for the first book and 75 cents for each additional book (Surface shipping may take three to four weeks)
________Air Mail or UPS: $3.50 for first book and 1$ for each additional

_____Payment:______________________________
_____Check______________________________

_____Credit card: _____ Visa, _____ MasterCard, _____ Optima, _____ AMEX.

Card number:______________________________

Name on card:__________________________ Exp. date:_____/______
program.

Sema Institute of Yoga P.O.Box 570459, Miami, Florida, 33257 (305) 378-6253